T0233275

Infrastructure-as-Code Automation Using Terraform, Packer, Vault, Nomad and Consul

Hands-on Deployment, Configuration, and Best Practices

Navin Sabharwal
Sarvesh Pandey
Piyush Pandey

Apress®

Infrastructure-as-Code Automation Using Terraform, Packer, Vault, Nomad and Consul: Hands-on Deployment, Configuration, and Best Practices

Navin Sabharwal
New Delhi, Delhi, India

Sarvesh Pandey
Noida, UP, India

Piyush Pandey
New Delhi, India

ISBN-13 (pbk): 978-1-4842-7128-5
https://doi.org/10.1007/978-1-4842-7129-2

ISBN-13 (electronic): 978-1-4842-7129-2

Copyright © 2021 by Navin Sabharwal, Sarvesh Pandey and Piyush Pandey

This work is subject to copyright. All rights are reserved by the Publisher, whether the whole or part of the material is concerned, specifically the rights of translation, reprinting, reuse of illustrations, recitation, broadcasting, reproduction on microfilms or in any other physical way, and transmission or information storage and retrieval, electronic adaptation, computer software, or by similar or dissimilar methodology now known or hereafter developed.

Trademarked names, logos, and images may appear in this book. Rather than use a trademark symbol with every occurrence of a trademarked name, logo, or image we use the names, logos, and images only in an editorial fashion and to the benefit of the trademark owner, with no intention of infringement of the trademark.

The use in this publication of trade names, trademarks, service marks, and similar terms, even if they are not identified as such, is not to be taken as an expression of opinion as to whether or not they are subject to proprietary rights.

While the advice and information in this book are believed to be true and accurate at the date of publication, neither the authors nor the editors nor the publisher can accept any legal responsibility for any errors or omissions that may be made. The publisher makes no warranty, express or implied, with respect to the material contained herein.

Managing Director, Apress Media LLC: Welmoed Spahr
Acquisitions Editor: Celestin Suresh John
Development Editor: Matthew Moodie
Coordinating Editor: Aditee Mirashi

Cover designed by eStudioCalamar

Cover image designed by Freepik (www.freepik.com)

Distributed to the book trade worldwide by Springer Science+Business Media New York, 1 New York Plaza, Suite 4600, New York, NY 10004-1562, USA. Phone 1-800-SPRINGER, fax (201) 348-4505, e-mail orders-ny@springer-sbm.com, or visit www.springeronline.com. Apress Media, LLC is a California LLC and the sole member (owner) is Springer Science + Business Media Finance Inc (SSBM Finance Inc). SSBM Finance Inc is a **Delaware** corporation.

For information on translations, please e-mail booktranslations@springernature.com; for reprint, paperback, or audio rights, please e-mail bookpermissions@springernature.com.

Apress titles may be purchased in bulk for academic, corporate, or promotional use. eBook versions and licenses are also available for most titles. For more information, reference our Print and eBook Bulk Sales web page at http://www.apress.com/bulk-sales.

Any source code or other supplementary material referenced by the author in this book is available to readers on GitHub via the book's product page, located at www.apress.com/ 978-1-4842-7128-5. For more detailed information, please visit http://www.apress.com/ source-code.

Printed on acid-free paper

Table of Contents

About the Authors

Navin Sabharwal has more than 20 years of industry experience. He is an innovator, thought leader, patent holder, and author in cloud computing, artificial intelligence and machine learning, public cloud, DevOps, AIOPS, infrastructure services, monitoring and management platforms, big data analytics, and software product development. Navin is responsible for DevOps, artificial intelligence, cloud lifecycle management, service management, monitoring and management, IT Ops analytics, AIOPs and machine learning, automation, operational efficiency of scaled delivery through lean Ops, strategy, and delivery for HCL Technologies. He can be reached at Navinsabharwal@gmail.com and www.linkedin.com/in/navinsabharwal.

Sarvesh Pandey is an innovator and thought leader in hybrid cloud lifecycle automation covering technologies (IP and OEM products) like cloud management automation, infrastructure as code, and Runbook Automation, with 15 years of IT experience. He is the Associate Director and Practice Head of Cloud Management Automation for HCL's DRYiCE, focusing on planning, designing, and managing multiple infrastructure automation projects of strategic importance to the cloud and the IAC framework. He has experience in working with highly engineered systems that require a deep understanding of cutting-edge technology and the key drivers in multiple markets. He can be reached at samsarvesh@gmail.com and https://in.linkedin.com/in/sarvesh-pandey-11b82717.

Piyush Pandey has 10+ years of Industry Experience. He is currently working at HCL Technologies as Automation Architect delivering solutions catering to Hybrid Cloud using Cloud Native and 3rd Party Solutions. The Automation solutions cover use cases like Enterprise Observability, Infra as Code, Server Automation. Runbook Automation, Cloud Management Platform, Cloud Native Automation and Dashboard/Visibility. He is responsible for designing end to end solutions & architecture for enterprise Automation adoption. piyushnsitcoep@gmail.com and https://www.linkedin.com/in/piyush-pandey-704495b.

About the Technical Reviewer

Santhosh Kumar Srinivasan is an AWS Certified Solutions Architect and TripleByte Certified DevOps Engineer in India. He works as a cloud consultant with Fortune 100 clients in the United States. He is an expert in architecting highly available, fault-tolerant workloads in AWS Cloud to solve complex problems. San is a mentor for advanced certification in software engineering for cloud, blockchain, and IOT offered by IIT Madras and GreatLearning. He has trained hundreds of developers on full stack development in Python.

He has a bachelor's degree in computer applications from Bharathiar University, Coimbatore. San creates and maintains open source teaching materials on various software engineering topics such as Python, AWS, and RegEx on his GitHub profile (`https://github.com/sanspace`). He lived in North Carolina and Virginia for four years before moving back to his hometown in Coimbatore, India, where he is currently living with his wife.

He is an avid user of Terraform and works with other Hashicorp products in his line of work. He plays chess, table tennis, and badminton. To know more about San, please visit his website at `https://sanspace.in` or follow him on Twitter @2sks (`https://twitter.com/2sks`).

Acknowledgments

To my family, Shweta and Soumil: for being always there by my side and letting me sacrifice their time for my intellectual and spiritual pursuits, and for taking care of everything while I am immersed in authoring. This and other accomplishments of my life wouldn't have been possible without your love and support.

To my mom and my sister: for their love and support as always; without your blessings, nothing is possible.

To my co-authors, Sarvesh and Piyush: thank you for the hard work and quick turnarounds to deliver this. It was an enriching experience, and I am looking forward to working with you again soon.

I want to send special thanks to Rohan Bajaj, Abhijeet Thakur, Manpreet Singh, Parvathy Subbiah, Tholupuluri Tsnmanindrababu, Aditya Tanwar, and Avinaw Sharma. Their research input and automation code samples helped in shaping the outline of the book.

To my team at HCL, who has been a source of inspiration with their hard work, ever engaging technical conversations, and technical depth: your everflowing ideas are a source of happiness and excitement every single day. Amit Agrawal, Vasand Kumar, Punith Krishnamurthy, Sandeep Sharma, Amit Dwivedi, Gauarv Bhardwaj, Nitin Narotra, and Vivek—thank you for being there and making technology fun.

Thank you to Celestine, Aditee, and the entire team at Apress for turning our ideas into reality. It has been an amazing experience authoring with you, and over the years, the speed of decision-making and the editorial support has been excellent.

To all that I have had the opportunity to work with my co-authors, colleagues, managers, mentors, and guides in this world of 7 billion people: it was a coincidence that brought us together. It is an enriching experience to be associated with you and learn from you. All ideas and paths are an assimilation of conversations that I have had and experiences I have shared. Thank you.

Thank you, goddess Saraswati, for guiding me to the path of knowledge and spirituality and keeping me on this path until salvation.

असतो मा साद गमय, तमसो मा ज्योतिर् गमय, मृत्योर मा अमृतम् गमय

(Asato Ma Sad Gamaya, Tamaso Ma Jyotir Gamaya, Mrityor Ma Amritam Gamaya)

Lead us from ignorance to truth, lead us from darkness to light, lead us from death to deathlessness.

CHAPTER 1

Getting Started with HashiCorp Automation Solutions

This chapter introduces you to infrastructure as code (IaC) and HashiCorp's automation offerings, helping users adopt the IaC philosophy to manage infrastructure and the application lifecycle. The chapter covers the following topics.

- Introduction to infrastructure as code
- Introduction to HashiCorp's automation offerings

Introduction to Infrastructure as Code

Building infrastructure is an evolving and complex art, which demands repetitive improvements involving aspects such as maintainability, scalability, fault-tolerance, and performance.

In traditional environment, building and deploying infrastructure components was a manual and tedious task which translates to delays and decreases organizational agility. With the emergence of IaC infra components are now treated as merely a software construct, a code which can be shared across different teams. IaC has given rise to mutable infrastructure as the

© Navin Sabharwal, Sarvesh Pandey and Piyush Pandey 2021
N. Sabharwal et al., *Infrastructure-as-Code Automation Using Terraform, Packer, Vault, Nomad and Consul*, https://doi.org/10.1007/978-1-4842-7129-2_1

lifecycle of every infra resource/component is treated via code. This leads to negligible configuration drift across various environments thereby maintaining sanity of the environment. Infrastructure is treated the same way an application is treated in an environment. It follows the same devops principle as application, shares same pipelines and is version controlled.

Another key benefit that IaC offers is the consistency of the build. If you need to manage several environments (e.g., development, QA, staging, and production), spinning those up from the same codebase ensures that negligible configuration drift is introduced across the environments, ensuring that they all behave the same way.

IaC encourages declarative style of code wherein the desired end state and the configuration are present before final state is provisioned. Declarative code tends to be more reusable in the environment as current configuration changes are considered while catering for any new request for new infrastructure.

Figure 1-1 is a high-level view of how IaC tools operate.

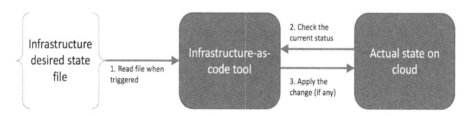

Figure 1-1. *How infrastructure as code works*

IaC solutions complies with below mentioned principles, as shown in Figure 1-2.

- **Version control** is a popular concept wherein every release corresponds to a source code build which is maintained as a versioned artifact in the environment. In IaC, a similar principle is applied to manage the infrastructure and changes using version-control commits in the source code repository. This provides traceability of changes made to the infrastructure definition covering who made changes, what has changed, and so forth. This is also crucial when you need to roll back to a previous version of the code while troubleshooting an issue.

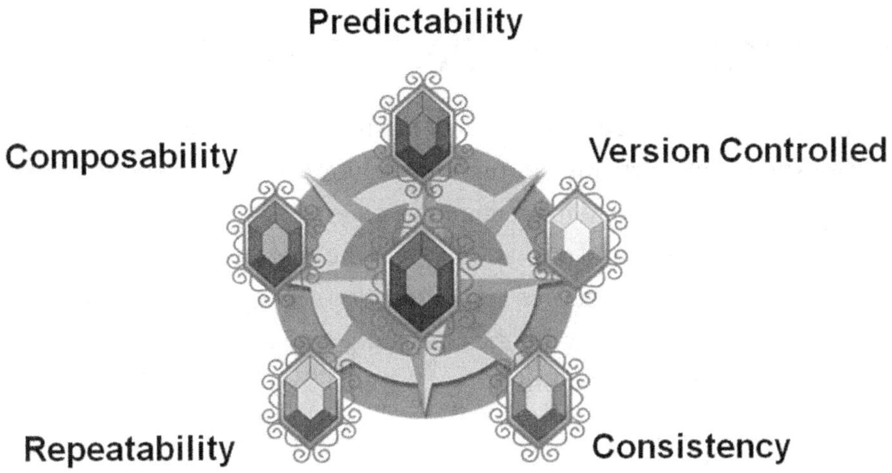

Figure 1-2. *Principles of infrastructure as code*

- **Predictability** refers to IaC capability as a solution to always provide the same environment and associated attributes (as defined in the version-controlled system) every time it is invoked.

- **Consistency** ensures that multiple instances of the same baseline code provide a similar environment. This avoids inconsistencies and configuration drift when manually building complex infrastructure entities.

- **Repeatability** refers to a solution that always provides the same results based on the provided input.

3

- **Composability** refers to service managed in a modular and abstracted format, which can be used to build complex application systems. This feature empowers users to focus on the target application build rather than worry about the under-the-hood details and complex logic used for provisioning.

Introduction to HashiCorp Automation

HashiCorp, founded in 2012 by Mitchell Hashimoto and Armon Dadgar, is a well known infrastructure automation solution company with the aim of automating hybrid cloud management processes, including application development, delivery, and operations. Over the years, HashiCorp has released a variety of open source and enterprise-supported hybrid cloud automation solutions. Below are the Hashicorp toolsets which are widely available for enterprise solutions–

- Terraform
- Vault
- Packer
- Consul
- Nomad
- Vagrant
- Boundary
- Waypoint

Now let's look at how each of these solutions enables hybrid cloud automation.

Packer

Image management has been a fundamental prerequisite for virtual or physical system provisioning. Traditional image automation solutions leverages baselines or golden images were manually build and maintained. However, human errors introduced at the image-build stage could lead to configuration drift in the provisioned service. HashiCorp Packer is an open source tool for creating golden images for multiple platforms from single source configuration thereby solving problems with manually created images.

Packer lets you automate the build of golden images. It works with tools like ansible to install software while creating images. It uses configuration files along with the concepts of builder and provisioners to spin up, configure an instance as a golden image. The configuration code can be changed in case of introduction of a new state element (addition of a new agent) or during updation scenarios (patching, hardening) of golden image and is used to create an updated image without human intervention.

The following are the key advantages of Packer solutions.

- **Accelerated image creation and update process**:
  Packer helps create and update multiple images
  belonging to multiple clouds or multiple OS types
  within minutes. You don't have to wait for the
  administrator to create/update manually, which can
  take hours or even days.

- **Support for multiple providers**: Packer supports
  multiple providers and platforms, so you can manage
  identical images across your hybrid cloud environment
  with the same standardization and consistency level.

- **Reduction in human error–induced inconsistencies**:
  Using a codified approach for managing images, you
  can remove any inconsistencies or configuration drifts
  in your environment.

5

Terraform

Terraform is an IaC (infrastructure as code) tool that allows users to define a desirable infrastructure definition in a declarative language. Using terraform the infra components within the environment can be deployed and treated as a code in terraform's configuration file that you can version, share and reuse.

HashiCorp Terraform has its own configuration language called HCL (HashiCorp Configuration Language). An HCL file always ends with *.tf. HashiCorp also supports the JSON format for configuration files. It's the user's decision on whether to use JSON or HCL to write Terraform code. HCL is widely used because of its simplicity and complex knowledge of target infrastructure technologies.

HashiCorp Terraform is available in the following three modes.

- Terraform CLI (open source)

- Terraform Cloud

- Terraform Enterprise

The following are the key benefits of using HashiCorp Terraform.

- **Accelerated hybrid cloud service provisioning**: Terraform enables accelerated provisioning of services across the hybrid cloud, covering more than 500 technologies.

- **State management**: Terraform allows tracking services for changes or configuration drifts. This enables governance of service configuration beyond the provisioning phase of the service lifecycle.

- **Planning and testing services**: Terraform enables the planning and testing of services before the provisioning or modification stages, allowing users to safely and predictably manage the service lifecycle.

- **Consistency and reduction in human errors**: Using a codified approach to managing the service lifecycle, you can remove any inconsistencies or configuration drifts in your environment.

Vault

HashiCorp Vault is leveraged for storing and securely accessing secrets via API keys and password. Secrets are defined as any form of sensitive credentials that need to be controlled; they are used to unlock sensitive information. Secrets can be stored in passwords, API keys, or SSH keys. Vault stores secrets for authentication and authorization.

Protecting secrets and access for automation is of primary importance. HashiCorp Vault solutions make it easy to manage secrets and access by leveraging the API and a user-friendly interface. You can monitor detailed logs and fetch audit trails on who accessed which secrets and when.

User authentication is via a password or by using dynamic values to generate temporary tokens that allow access to a particular path. Policies can also be defined using HCL to determine which user gets what level of access.

Nomad

HashiCorp Nomad is an easy-to-use workload manager that enables users to schedule tasks and deploy applications in a containerized or non-containerized infrastructure. It allows you to write code and build software using declarative infrastructure as code.

Consul

HashiCorp Consul is a multiple–data center service mesh solution that provides the capability to govern application service communication using a control plane. It also offers service discovery and health checks. It leverages a secure TLS protocol to establish mutual TLS connections.

A service mesh allows you to control communication between different application components or between multiple applications. A service mesh leverages the IaC concept to define a communication policy. It typically uses a network proxy or sidecar concept for governing communication between application services. Data communication patterns help developers optimize service interaction and performance. For example, a service mesh can monitor the amount of time it takes to reconnect to access the application service during unavailability. This can help developers redefine the waiting period before an application service tries to reconnect.

Vagrant

One of the fundamental challenges developers face is the consistency of the development environment used for writing code. Multiple solutions are available on the market, including VirtualBox, VMware Workstation, and Docker. Hypervisor platforms like VMware, KVM, and Hyper-V are typically used for setting up developer workstations; however, manual administration makes it tedious to manage configuration requirements for each application team which results in no consistency between different environments and introduces configuration drift due to manual intervention.

HashiCorp Vagrant enables you to build and manage a developer's environment using a workflow-driven approach that leverages the power of infrastructure as a code. Using its integrations with various platform technologies, the developer environment is configured using a consistent, repeatable, and accelerated approach. From a developer's perspective,

all the required software, utilities, and environment configurations
can be applied to the environment using Vagrant's file configuration. It
enables application team members to use the same standard platform for
development.

Vagrant is supported on multiple platforms, enabling developers to
focus on development using their favorite software and tools without
worrying about the underlying platform.

Boundary

In modern times, especially in the wake of COVID-19, there is a paradigm
shift toward identity-based access. With most businesses, applications,
and infrastructure users working remotely, organizations cannot rely on
a network perimeter to secure access to resources. HashiCorp Boundary
provides identity-based access to resources by using popular identity
providers for authentication and authorization to human users.

Using integration with popular identity providers like Microsoft Azure
Active Directory, Okta, and PingFederate for authentication, Boundary
enables role-based authorized access to target services. This removes the
dependency of tracking the end user by using a physical IP address. User
access can now be defined using policies stored in a version-controlled
system, ensuring secure access to hybrid cloud services and applications
with automated governance.

Waypoint

As modern infrastructure becomes more complex with the rise of public
cloud IaaS and PaaS services and container/microservice/serverless-
based applications, it's difficult for developers to keep track of deployment
approaches in every platform (VM-based configurations, YAML files,
Kubectl, schedulers, etc.). HashiCorp Waypoint enables developers to
define the flow of how an application is built, deployed, and released

across platforms. Waypoint is not a package manager or replacement of solutions like Kubernetes. It enables the abstraction of build and deployment complexities using codified flow, which is versioned controlled.

Waypoint leverages build packs to build applications for various languages and frameworks, which can be stored as artifacts. These artifacts can be deployed on various platforms, leveraging either IaaS or PaaS services. With a Waypoint solution, you can create a workflow to deploy application components that use other solutions from HashiCorp, such as Packer (for defining baseline image), Terraform (for defining desired state configuration), Vault (for managing secrets), Nomad (for application orchestration), or Consul (for managing Service to service connectivity).

Summary

This chapter introduced infrastructure as code and various automation solutions from HashiCorp that leverage the IaC principle. Upcoming chapters cover Terraform, Packer, Vault, Nomad, and Consul and how these solutions can be used in hybrid cloud automation.

CHAPTER 2

Getting Started with HashiCorp Terraform

This chapter covers the core concepts of Terraform CLI and Terraform Cloud automation.

- Introduction to HashiCorp Terraform
- Setting up an AWS account
- Getting started with Terraform Cloud
- Getting started with Terraform CLI

Introduction to HashiCorp Terraform

DevOps and infrastructure as code (IaC) are gaining traction globally with developers, administrators, architects, and cloud engineers. DevOps is a philosophy encompassing people, processes, and tools. Its objective is to accelerate software development and associated release and deployment processes. In the overall umbrella of DevOps, IaC is an important component that provides agility and scalability from the infrastructure side to meet a application team's needs. Infrastructure as code also enables stable, secure, and consistent platforms for hosting applications.

© Navin Sabharwal, Sarvesh Pandey and Piyush Pandey 2021
N. Sabharwal et al., *Infrastructure-as-Code Automation Using Terraform, Packer, Vault, Nomad and Consul*, https://doi.org/10.1007/978-1-4842-7129-2_2

There are many tools that implement infrastructure as code. Terraform and Ansible are gaining traction in the DevOps and developer communities. Similarly, public cloud hosting platforms provide native solutions packaged as part of public cloud service offerings. This includes AWS CloudFormation and Azure Resource Manager. In Google Cloud Platform, the cloud-native IaC offering is called a *deployment manager*.

Terraform is an IaC tool that allows users to build, manage, and version their infrastructures efficiently.

At a high level, Terraform consists of the following components.

- Hashicorp Terraform has its own configuration language called HCL (HashiCorp Configuration Language). Each configuration file may consists of multiple code blocks wherein each codeblock corresponds to an infra resource in the environment. HashiCorp also supports creation of configuration files in JSON format. HCL defines infrastructure in a declarative language. Declarative languages are nonprocedural or high level language, which specifies what is to be done rather than how to do it.

  Terraform understands HCL as the default configuration language. It identifies HCL file by its .tf extension. For the ease of end users, terraform can also read JSON-based configuration files. It's up to the user to use JSON or HCL for writing Terraform code.

  HCL is widely used for its simplicity and complex knowledge of target infrastructure technologies.

- A **workspace** determines how terraform organizes infrastructure. It contains everything terraform needs to manage a given collection of infrastructure and separate workspaces corresponds to separate working directories. Every workspace has a configuration file and an associated backend configuration that defines how the deployment was executed and where a state was captured for deployment. Initially, there is only a default workspace available; hence, all configurations are mapped to the default workspace. Additional workspaces can be created and switched to differentiate runs and configurations.

- A **workflow** is the way you manage and run your code in VCS or CLI. It consists of five major steps: write, initiate, plan, apply, and destroy. Terraform governs a resource service lifecycle through these five steps.

HashiCorp Terraform is available in the following three modes.

- Terraform CLI (open source)

- Terraform Cloud

- Terraform Enterprise

Let's look at each of these options.

Terraform CLI (Open Source)

Terraform CLI is an IaC tool released under Mozilla Public License 2.0, which is an open source license available to all. You can download the latest binaries from HashiCorp's repository according to the operating system of your choice and start using them to automate your use cases. Terraform CLI is recommended for users working on IaC projects, proof of concept, prototyping, or small noncritical applications.

Terraform Cloud

Terraform Cloud is one of HashiCorp's managed commercial SaaS offerings. You must subscribe to use it. The graphical user interface is user-friendly and offers a good platform for collaboration. HashiCorp provides a free account with limited offerings. Paid-subscription users have access to many additional features that the open source and evaluation versions don't have.

Terraform Cloud is best suited for users who want to leverage enterprise security controls like RBAC (role-based access control), team collaboration, REST, or RESTful API (representational state transfer API) interfaces for secure integration with other applications, without having to manage the underlying Terraform infrastructure.

Terraform Enterprise

Terraform Enterprise is HashiCorp's commercial version that allows you to host it locally in your own hosting space and have complete control over the infrastructure and management policies. Organizations with security or compliance concerns and that want to privately manage all aspects should opt for Terraform Enterprise.

Comparing the Options

Table 2-1 is a high-level comparison of all three HashiCorp Terraform offerings.

Table 2-1. *Comparison of Terraform (open source) vs. Terraform Cloud and Enterprise (paid versions)*

Feature	Terraform (open source)	Terraform Enterprise or Cloud	Feature Functionality (description)
Workspaces	Yes, but very limited functionality	Yes, with advanced capabilities	Teams map responsibility to individual workspaces and link APIs accordingly
Team Management	Difficult	Easy, well managed	Manages organizations, teams, and permissions separately
Private Module Registry	No	Yes	Private and central repository of modules
Configuration Designer	No	Yes	GUI to manage workspaces, variables, audits, and so forth
Sentinel	No	Yes	Enforces user-defined policies to better manage resources
SAML	No	Yes	SAML and SSO integration for easy authentication
Audit	No	Yes	Historical changes checked

Terraform Enterprise and Terraform Cloud offer the same level of functionality. As part of the Enterprise offering, this book provides a detailed walkthrough of usage for Terraform Cloud because it does not need any underlying infrastructure.

At a high level, Terraform consists of the following components.

- Terraform code for defining resources

- A workspace to logically manage Terraform configurations

- A workflow to manage your code in VCS and execute your code in CLI

Setting up an AWS Account

Before setting up Terraform, let's quickly set up an AWS account, which is used later in this chapter. We assume that you have basic knowledge of the three public clouds (Amazon Web Services (AWS), Azure, and Google Cloud Platform (GCP)) because the hands-on exercises in this book require it.

Navigate to https://portal.aws.amazon.com/billing/signup#/ start to create your AWS account. If you already have an AWS account, you can skip this exercise and proceed to the next one. Enter the required information as highlighted in Figure 2-1, and click the Continue button.

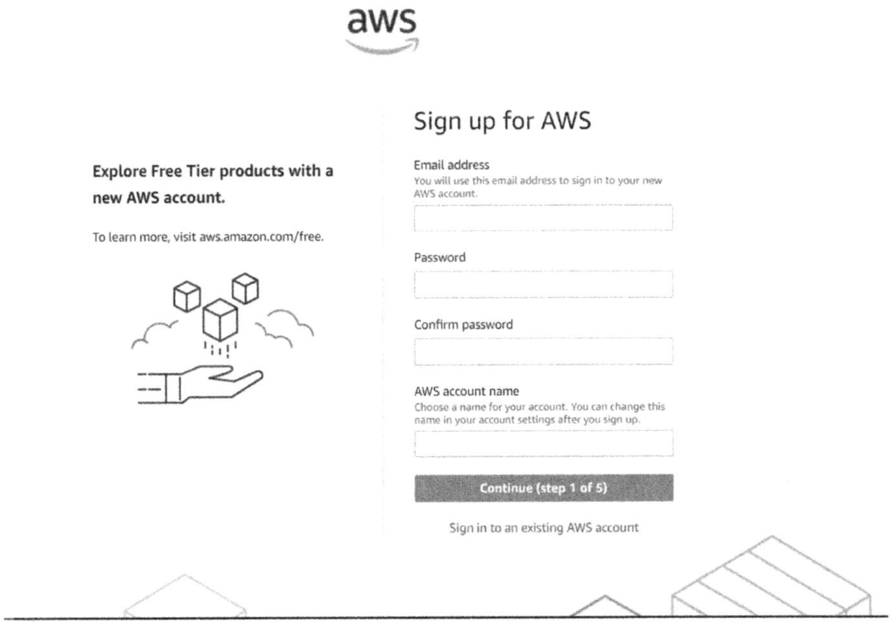

Sign up for AWS

Explore Free Tier products with a new AWS account.

To learn more, visit aws.amazon.com/free.

Email address
You will use this email address to sign in to your new AWS account.

Password

Confirm password

AWS account name
Choose a name for your account. You can change this name in your account settings after you sign up.

Continue (step 1 of 5)

Sign in to an existing AWS account

Figure 2-1. *New AWS Account registration page*

Select a personal account and enter your information. Click the Continue button (see Figure 2-2).

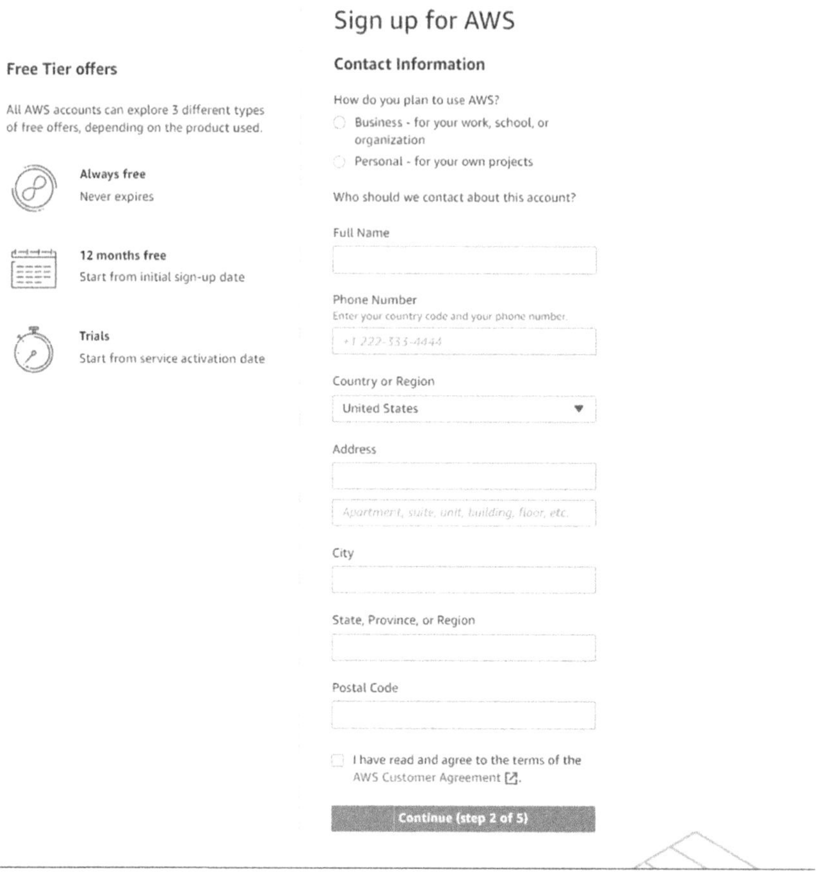

Figure 2-2. *Enter contact details*

Enter your payment information (see Figure 2-3). Click the Verify and Continue button.

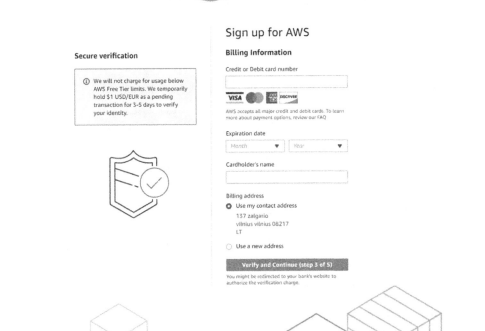

Figure 2-3. *Enter basic personal details*

Select the Basic Plan. For new users, this free plan is sufficient. Click the Free button (see Figure 2-4).

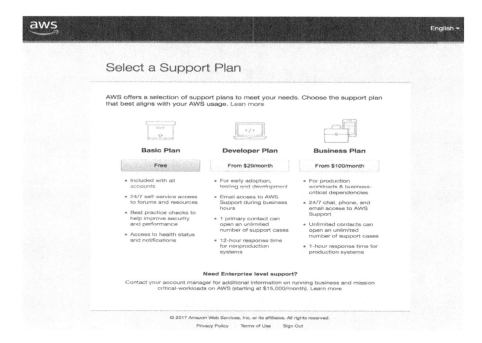

Figure 2-4. *Select free basic plan*

After successfully registering, log in to your AWS account (`https://console.aws.amazon.com/iam/home?region=us-east-1`) to access the AWS console.

Navigate to IAM ➤ Access management ➤ Users. Click the Add User button (see Figure 2-5).

Enter the relevant information (see Figure 2-6) and select programmatic access. When this is done, you get an access key and a secret key, which are used later in the exercise.

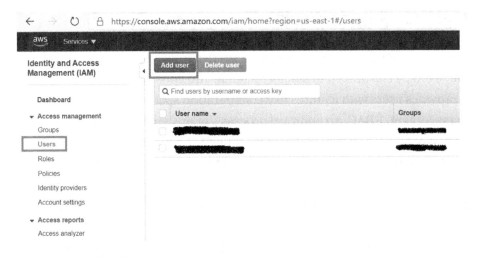

Figure 2-5. *IAM new user*

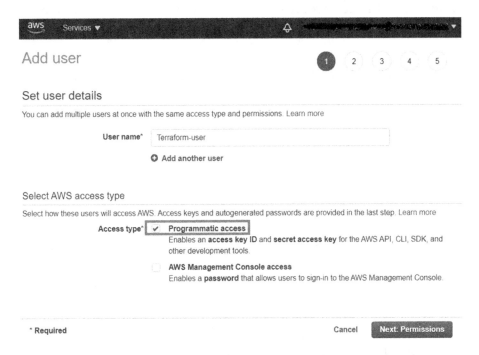

Figure 2-6. *Create new user with programmatic access*

Getting Started with Terraform Cloud

Terraform Cloud is a SaaS (software as service) offering. It is hosted and managed by HashiCorp in a highly reliable and consistent environment. It provides users with features like collaboration space, secret data management, RBAC, an approval process (for any changes), and a privately hosted registry to share Terraform modules and for policy control.

Terraform Cloud can be accessed at `https://app.terraform.io`. All you have to do is create a free account that allows collaboration in a small team and other features. Let's start with a hands-on exercise on subscribing to Terraform Cloud.

Create a new account on Terraform cloud using an email account of your choice by navigating to `https://app.terraform.io/signup/account`. Click Create a Free Account and provide information to create your account (see Figure 2-7).

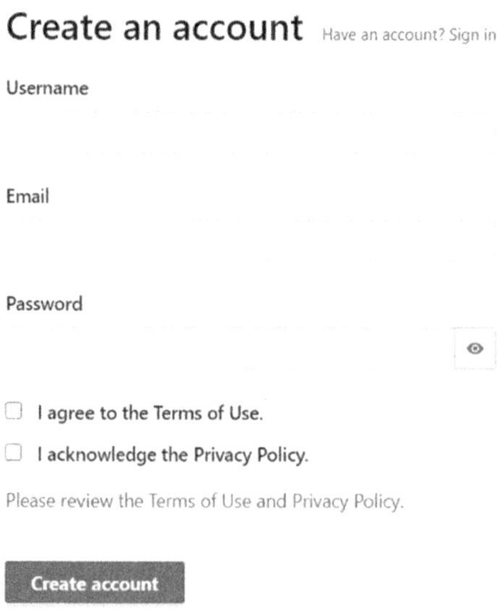

Create an account   Have an account? Sign in

Username

Email

Password

☐ I agree to the Terms of Use.
☐ I acknowledge the Privacy Policy.
Please review the Terms of Use and Privacy Policy.

Create account

Figure 2-7. *Terraform Cloud signup page*

As soon as you register on the Terraform Cloud site, you get a confirmation email from HashiCorp to verify your account. Click the link to confirm your email address (see Figure 2-8).

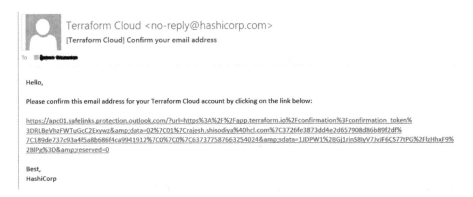

Figure 2-8. *New user registration verification email*

After email verification, you are redirected to a page that asks you to log in. Then, you are redirected to the Terraform Cloud, as shown in Figure 2-9. Select the Start from Scratch option.

Welcome to Terraform Cloud!

Choose your setup workflow

> **Try an example configuration**   Recommended for OSS users
>
> Perform your first Terraform Cloud run using a sample configuration with the CLI.   ›
>
> Learn More

> **Start from scratch**
>
> Start with a blank slate. Best for users who are already familiar with Terraform Cloud.   ›
>
> Learn More

Figure 2-9. *Terraform Cloud*

Create a new organization, as shown in Figure 2-10.

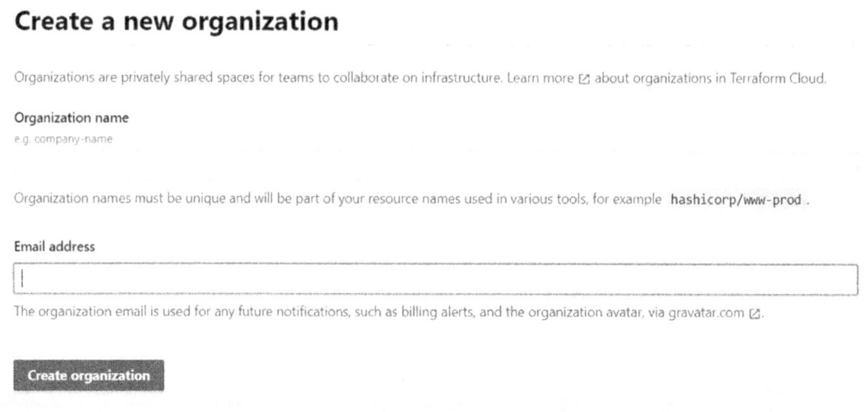

Create a new organization

Organizations are privately shared spaces for teams to collaborate on infrastructure. Learn more ☑ about organizations in Terraform Cloud.

Organization name
e.g. company-name

Organization names must be unique and will be part of your resource names used in various tools, for example `hashicorp/www-prod` .

Email address

The organization email is used for any future notifications, such as billing alerts, and the organization avatar, via gravatar.com ☑.

`Create organization`

Figure 2-10. *Terraform Cloud new organization*

Create a new workspace, as shown in Figure 2-11.

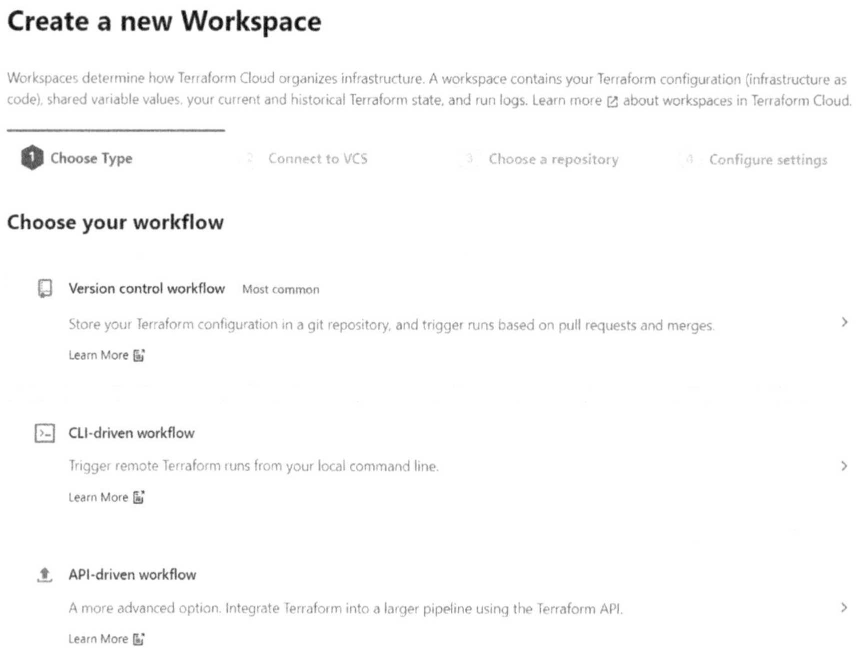

Create a new Workspace

Workspaces determine how Terraform Cloud organizes infrastructure. A workspace contains your Terraform configuration (infrastructure as code), shared variable values, your current and historical Terraform state, and run logs. Learn more ☑ about workspaces in Terraform Cloud.

1 Choose Type   2 Connect to VCS   3 Choose a repository   4 Configure settings

Choose your workflow

Version control workflow   Most common

Store your Terraform configuration in a git repository, and trigger runs based on pull requests and merges.   ⟩
Learn More 🔗

CLI-driven workflow

Trigger remote Terraform runs from your local command line.   ⟩
Learn More 🔗

API-driven workflow

A more advanced option. Integrate Terraform into a larger pipeline using the Terraform API.   ⟩
Learn More 🔗

Figure 2-11. *Terraform Cloud new workspace*

Terraform provides a workspace that makes it easy to manage code as things grow and become more complex. It's a place where you put your Terraform code and configurations. A new user might put all his code in a single work directory, which might grow over time, and he makes different directory structures for each environment or project. At some point, it becomes difficult to manage and change, and the chance for error grows. This is where a workspace comes in handy; it provides a logical separation of code rather than managing it in a complex directory structure.

Select a workflow from the three options. VCS (version-control system) is the most commonly used and preferred. It enables users to leverage GitOps-based actions to manage an infrastructure by using an IaC methodology. (Read more about VCS integration at `www.terraform.io/docs/cloud/vcs/`).

Let's select one of the VCS providers from the four provider options. We opted for GitLab, as shown in Figure 2-12.

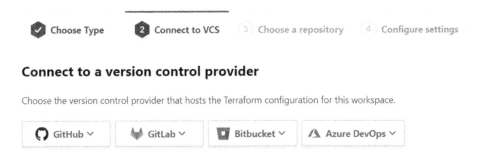

Figure 2-12. *Terraform Cloud VCS*

Select one of the GitLab provider options (see Figure 2-13). Go to User Settings ➤ Applications to add GitLab as the VCS provider.

Figure 2-13. *Add VCS provider in Terraform Cloud*

The following information is needed to use a GitLab provider (see Figure 2-14).

- Name

- Redirect URI

- Scopes (API only)

Terraform-CloudDemo / Settings / VCS Providers / Add VCS Provider

Add VCS Provider

To connect workspaces, modules, and policy sets to git repositories containing Terraform configurations, Terraform Cloud needs access to your version control system (VCS) provider. Use this page to configure OAuth authentication with your VCS provider. For more information, please see the Terraform Cloud documentation on Configuring Version Control Access ☑.

✅ Connect to VCS   ② Set up provider   ③ Set up SSH keypair

Set up provider

For additional information about connecting to GitLab.com to Terraform Cloud, please read our documentation ☑.

1. On GitLab, register a new OAuth Application. ☑ Enter the following information:

Name:	Terraform Cloud (Terraform-CloudDemo) ⎘ Copied!
Redirect URI:	https://app.terraform.io/auth/2eee91d0-600c-41f3-af4f-████447a99e/callback ⎘ Copied!
Scopes:	Only the following should be checked: api

2. After clicking the "Save application" button, you'll be taken to the new application's page. Enter the Application ID and Secret below:

Figure 2-14. *Add VCS with GitLab*

Log in to your GitLab account. Navigate to the User Settings page, and select Applications (see Figure 2-15). Enter the following information (see Figure 2-14).

- Name (a relevant friendly name)

- Redirect URI (unique to each cloud user)

- Scopes (check API)

27

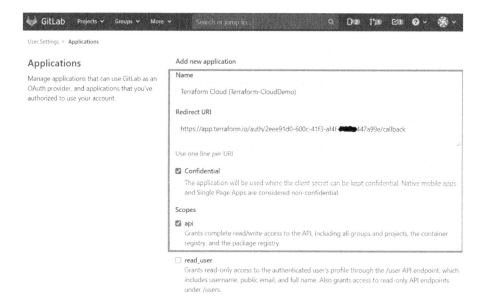

Figure 2-15. *GitLab application config to integrate GitLab with Terraform Cloud*

Once you save, enter the following information (see Figure 2-16).

- Application ID
- Secret

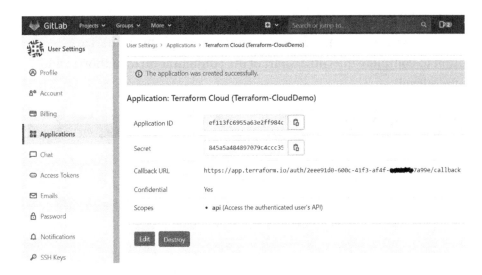

Figure 2-16. *GitLab application configuration for GitLab &*
Terraform integration

Navigate back to the Terraform Cloud page and enter the information
from GitLab (see Figure 2-16). Paste it in the Name, Application ID, and
Secret fields (see Figure 2-17).

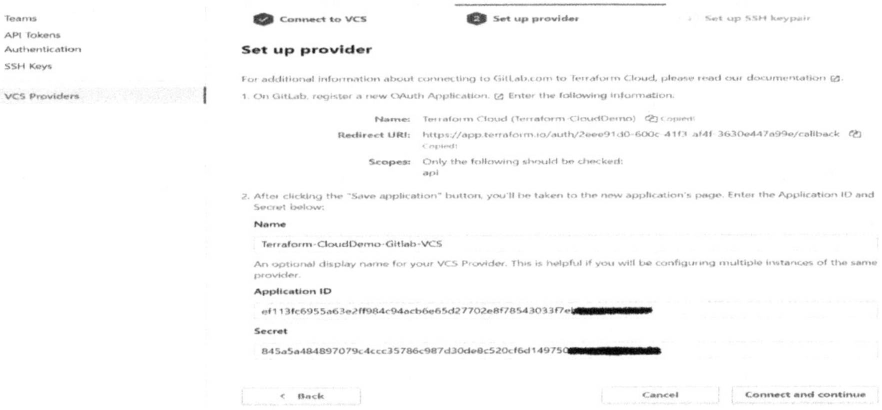

Figure 2-17. *Terraform Cloud Setup provider (with GitLab)*

Click the Connect and Continue button (see Figure 2-17), which takes you to the GitLab page (see Figure 2-18). Click the Authorize button to complete the GitLab part of the configuration to authorize and authenticate.

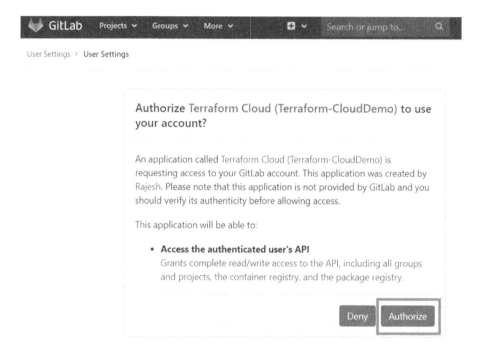

Figure 2-18. *GitLab Configured for Cloud User*

Click the Skip and Finish button (see Figure 2-19) to complete all VCS integration steps.

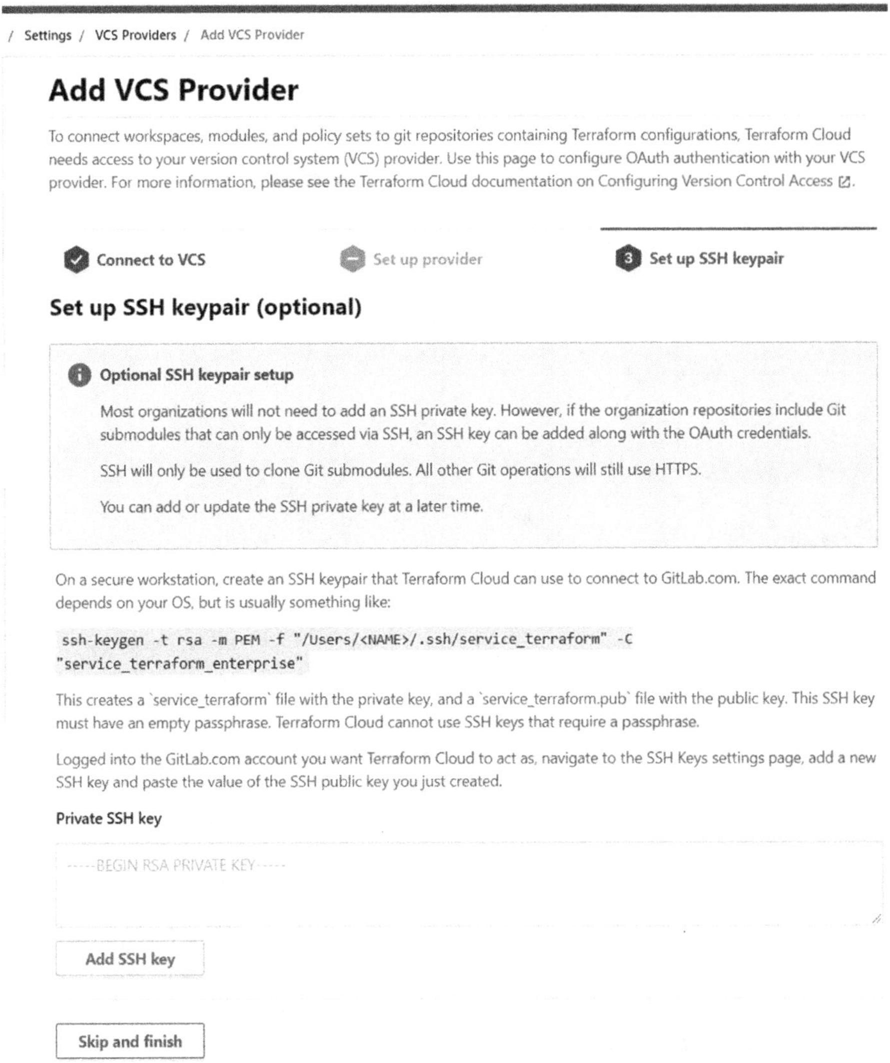

/ Settings / VCS Providers / Add VCS Provider

Add VCS Provider

To connect workspaces, modules, and policy sets to git repositories containing Terraform configurations, Terraform Cloud needs access to your version control system (VCS) provider. Use this page to configure OAuth authentication with your VCS provider. For more information, please see the Terraform Cloud documentation on Configuring Version Control Access ☑.

✓ Connect to VCS   ⊖ Set up provider   ③ Set up SSH keypair

Set up SSH keypair (optional)

ⓘ **Optional SSH keypair setup**

Most organizations will not need to add an SSH private key. However, if the organization repositories include Git submodules that can only be accessed via SSH, an SSH key can be added along with the OAuth credentials.

SSH will only be used to clone Git submodules. All other Git operations will still use HTTPS.

You can add or update the SSH private key at a later time.

On a secure workstation, create an SSH keypair that Terraform Cloud can use to connect to GitLab.com. The exact command depends on your OS, but is usually something like:

```
ssh-keygen -t rsa -m PEM -f "/Users/<NAME>/.ssh/service_terraform" -C
"service_terraform_enterprise"
```

This creates a `service_terraform` file with the private key, and a `service_terraform.pub` file with the public key. This SSH key must have an empty passphrase. Terraform Cloud cannot use SSH keys that require a passphrase.

Logged into the GitLab.com account you want Terraform Cloud to act as, navigate to the SSH Keys settings page, add a new SSH key and paste the value of the SSH public key you just created.

Private SSH key

```
-----BEGIN RSA PRIVATE KEY-----
```

Add SSH key

Skip and finish

Figure 2-19. *Add SSH and finish*

You should see the final page of the Terraform Cloud configuration (see Figure 2-20), which summarizes the authorization details.

Now you can use GitLab as the VCS for Terraform Cloud.

31

Figure 2-20. *Terraform Cloud integrated with GitLab as VCS summary*

Terraform Workflow

Once you log in with an activated Terraform Cloud account, you can start using a Terraform workflow. Workflows allow you to manage your code on a cloud platform. Terraform Cloud has the following three workflows for managing Terraform runs.

- **Version control workflow**: This workflow stores your Terraform configuration in a version-controlled system like Git or GitLab repository, and triggers runs based on pull and merges requests. It is one of the most commonly used approaches in Enterprise.

- **CLI-driven workflow**: In this approach, you can trigger remote Terraform runs from your local command line (CLI). Users can run CLI commands like `terraform plan` and `terraform apply`. They execute directly in Terraform Cloud. The user can monitor progress on a CLI terminal. This empowers developers and enforces the appropriate governances and policies offered by Terraform Enterprise.

- **API-driven workflow**: This is a more advanced option that integrates Terraform into a larger pipeline using the Terraform API.

As soon as you log in to your Terraform Cloud account, you are asked to choose one of three workflow options (see Figure 2-21).

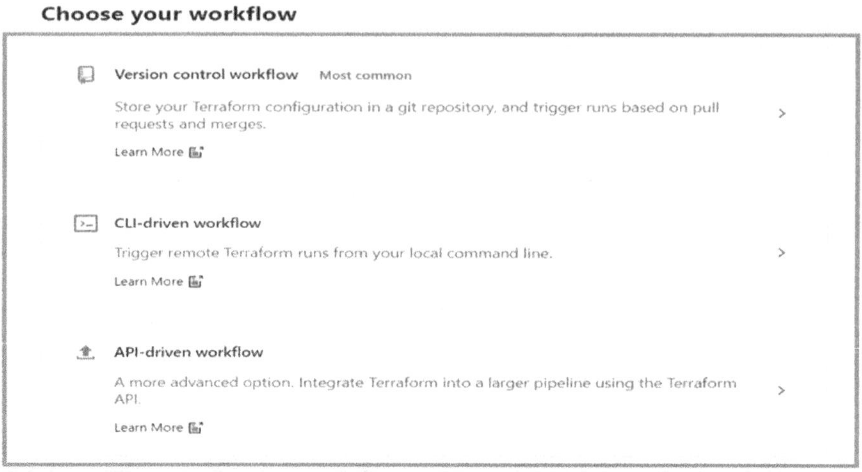

Choose your workflow

Figure 2-21. Terraform Cloud workflow

Getting Started with Terraform CLI

The previous section covered configuring Terraform Cloud and working with HashiCorp's Enterprise offerings. This section starts with HashiCorp's open source offering by configuring Terraform CLI on a Linux system. Our example uses a Red Hat virtual machine to install CLI.

Before you can download and configure Terraform, you need the wget and unzip tools on your virtual machine. Execute the following command to install packages on your virtual machine, as shown in Figure 2-22.

```
sudo yum install wget unzip -y
```

```
root@ ~]$  sudo yum install wget unzip -y
Loaded plugins: fastestmirror
Loading mirror speeds from cached hostfile
 * base: d36uatko69830t.cloudfront.net
 * epel: dl.fedoraproject.org
 * extras: d36uatko69830t.cloudfront.net
 * updates: d36uatko69830t.cloudfront.net
Resolving Dependencies
--> Running transaction check
---> Package unzip.x86_64 0:6.0-21.el7 will be installed
---> Package wget.x86_64 0:1.14-18.el7_6.1 will be installed
--> Finished Dependency Resolution

Dependencies Resolved

================================================================================
 Package            Arch            Version            Repository          Size
================================================================================
Installing:
 unzip              x86_64          6.0-21.el7         base               171 k
 wget               x86_64          1.14-18.el7_6.1    base               547 k

Transaction Summary
================================================================================
Install  2 Packages
```

Figure 2-22. *Prerequisite tool install*

Download a Terraform binary from the Terraform release website by executing the following command based on your computer's architecture and operating system platform (Linux, Windows, etc.). We used version 0.13 for our installation (see Figure 2-23).

sudo wget https://releases.hashicorp.com/terraform/0.13.5/
terraform_0.13.5_linux_amd64.zip

Note   Always refrain from downloading an application binary from third-party sites; only use the HashiCorp Terraform official release.

```
[root@ ~]$ sudo wget https://releases.hashicorp.com/terraform/0.13.5/terraform_0.13.5_linux_amd64.zip
--2020-10-27 10:22:04--  https://releases.hashicorp.com/terraform/0.13.5/terraform_0.13.5_linux_amd64.zip
Resolving releases.hashicorp.com (releases.hashicorp.com)... 151.101.249.183, 2a04:4e42:2f::439
Connecting to releases.hashicorp.com (releases.hashicorp.com)|151.101.249.183|:443... connected.
HTTP request sent, awaiting response... 200 OK
Length: 34880173 (33M) [application/zip]
Saving to: àterraform_0.13.5_linux_amd64.zipÅ

100%[===================================================================>] 34,880,173  --.-K/s   in 0.1s
```

Figure 2-23. *Terraform CLI download*

Use the following Linux command to unpack/unzip the binary you downloaded from the official Terraform website (see Figure 2-24).

sudo unzip terraform_0.13.5_linux_amd64.zip

```
[root@ ~]$ sudo unzip terraform_0.13.5_linux_amd64.zip
Archive:   terraform_0.13.5_linux_amd64.zip
  inflating: terraform
[root@ ~]$ ll
total 438536
-rwxr-xr-x 1 root       root       85545059 Oct 21 18:50 terraform
```

Figure 2-24. *Unzip Terraform binary*

Once the Terraform binary unzips in the current directory, you can place it in the location where all other system binaries reside. No path has to be configured to invoke Terraform CLI.

```
sudo mv terraform /usr/local/bin/
```

Execute the following command to validate that you have installed the correct version, as shown in Figure 2-25.

```
terraform version
```

```
[root@ ~]$ sudo mv terraform /usr/local/bin/
[root@ ~]$ terraform version
Terraform v0.13.5
```

Figure 2-25. *Configure Terraform*

Now that Terraform CLI is installed, let's test some Terraform code to see how things work.

Execute the following commands to install the Git client, and then clone the sample code from the GitHub repository.

```
yum install git
git clone https://github.com/dryice-devops/terraform_aws.git
```

Once you have cloned the repository, you should see five Terraform files (see Listing 2-1 through Listing 2-5).

Listing 2-1. Terraform data.tf File

```
data "aws_ami" "centos" {
  owners      = ["679593333241"]
  most_recent = true
  filter {
    name   = "name"
    values = ["CentOS Linux 7 x86_64 HVM EBS *"]
  }
  filter {
    name   = "architecture"
    values = ["x86_64"]
  }
  filter {
    name   = "root-device-type"
    values = ["ebs"]
  }
}
```

Listing 2-2. Terraform main.tf File

```
resource "aws_instance" "instance" {
  ami                          = data.aws_ami.centos.id
  instance_type                = var.Instancetype
  associate_public_ip_address = "true"
  monitoring                   = "true"
  key_name = var.key_name
  subnet_id   = var.subnet_id
  vpc_security_group_ids = var.vpc_security_group_ids
```

```
tags = {
    Name = var.name
    Environment = var.environment
    Business_Justification = var.bJustification
    Reason = var.reason
    }
```

Listing 2-3. Terraform output.tf File

```
output "instance_ips" {
  value = ["${aws_instance.instance.*.private_ip}"]
}
```

Listing 2-4. Terraform provider.tf File

```
provider "aws" {
access_key     = var.aws_accesskey
secret_key    = var.aws_secretkey
region             = var.region
}
```

Listing 2-5. Terraform variable.tf

```
variable "aws_accesskey" {
default   = "ASIA3WEU6XXXXXXXXXXXXX"
description       = "Enter Access Key"
}
variable "aws_secretkey" {
default = "bzNmvUZvsdidkhJzXXXXXXXXXXXXXXXXXXXXXXXXXXXX"
description = "Enter Secrete Key"
}
variable "environment" {
default = "development"
}
```

```
variable "vpc_security_group_ids"{
  description = "security group"
  type        = list(string)
  default =[]
}
variable "subnet_id" {
  description = "Subnet ID"
}
variable "bJustification" {
default = "Demo"
}
variable "reason" {
default = "Demo FOr Customer"
}
variable "name" {
  description = "Creates a unique name beginning with the
                specified prefix"
}
variable "Instancetype" {
  description = "The size of instance to launch"
}

variable "key_name" {
  description = "The key name that should be used for the
                instance"
  default     = ""
}
```

After cloning the code from the repository, you need to modify the information in your AWS account. Once the code is modified, you can start the Terraform initialization by executing the following command (see Figure 2-26).

```
terraform init
```

```
[vcs@ terra]$  ll
total 8
-rw-rw-r-- 1 root root 402 Nov  5 08:41 main.tf
-rw-rw-r-- 1 root root 220 Nov  5 08:39 variable.tf
[vcs@ terra]$
[vcs@ terra]$  terraform init

Initializing the backend...

Initializing provider plugins...
- Finding latest version of hashicorp/aws...
- Installing hashicorp/aws v3.13.0...
- Installed hashicorp/aws v3.13.0 (signed by HashiCorp)

The following providers do not have any version constraints in configuration,
so the latest version was installed.

To prevent automatic upgrades to new major versions that may contain breaking
changes, we recommend adding version constraints in a required_providers block
in your configuration, with the constraint strings suggested below.

* hashicorp/aws: version = "~> 3.13.0"

Terraform has been successfully initialized!

You may now begin working with Terraform. Try running "terraform plan" to see
any changes that are required for your infrastructure. All Terraform commands
should now work.

If you ever set or change modules or backend configuration for Terraform,
rerun this command to reinitialize your working directory. If you forget, other
commands will detect it and remind you to do so if necessary.
[vcs@ terra]$
```

Figure 2-26. *Terraform code clone and run*

Now you can apply as shown in Figure 2-27 the Terraform changes
using the following command, which starts provisioning the resources on
the AWS public cloud.

```
terraform apply
```

```
[vcs@ terra]$  terraform apply

An execution plan has been generated and is shown below.
Resource actions are indicated with the following symbols:
  + create

Terraform will perform the following actions:

  # aws_instance.ec2_server will be created
  + resource "aws_instance" "ec2_server" {
      + ami                          = "ami-0947d2ba12ee1ff75"
      + arn                          = (known after apply)
      + associate_public_ip_address  = (known after apply)
      + availability_zone            = (known after apply)
      + cpu_core_count               = (known after apply)
      + cpu_threads_per_core         = (known after apply)
      + get_password_data            = false
      + host_id                      = (known after apply)
      + id                           = (known after apply)
      + instance_state               = (known after apply)
      + instance_type                = "t2.micro"
      + ipv6_address_count           = (known after apply)
      + ipv6_addresses               = (known after apply)
      + key_name                     = (known after apply)
      + outpost_arn                  = (known after apply)
      + password_data                = (known after apply)
      + placement_group              = (known after apply)
      + primary_network_interface_id = (known after apply)
      + private_dns                  = (known after apply)
      + private_ip                   = (known after apply)
      + public_dns                   = (known after apply)
      + public_ip                    = (known after apply)
      + secondary_private_ips        = (known after apply)
      + security_groups              = (known after apply)
      + source_dest_check            = true
      + subnet_id                    = (known after apply)
      + tags                         = {
          + "Environment" = "MyDemo"
          + "Name"        = "My_EC2_host"
        }
```

Figure 2-27. Terraform apply

The `terraform apply` command initially runs a Terraform plan to validate the deployment and resources created as a part of the deployment. Once the plan is successful, it seeks an interactive user confirmation to proceed with the actual resource creation. This is done by typing YES in the interactive shell. However, if you need to suppress the prompt, you can use the –auto-approve flag along with terraform apply.

Once apply completes, you should see the output shown in Figure 2-28, which includes the number of resources added, changed, or destroyed to meet the changes defined in our Terraform code.

```
      + root_block_device {
          + delete_on_termination = (known after apply)
          + device_name           = (known after apply)
          + encrypted             = (known after apply)
          + iops                  = (known after apply)
          + kms_key_id            = (known after apply)
          + volume_id             = (known after apply)
          + volume_size           = (known after apply)
          + volume_type           = (known after apply)
        }
    }

Plan: 1 to add, 0 to change, 0 to destroy.

Do you want to perform these actions?
  Terraform will perform the actions described above.
  Only 'yes' will be accepted to approve.

  Enter a value: yes

aws_instance.ec2_server: Creating...
aws_instance.ec2_server: Still creating... [10s elapsed]
aws_instance.ec2_server: Still creating... [20s elapsed]
aws_instance.ec2_server: Still creating... [30s elapsed]
aws_instance.ec2_server: Still creating... [40s elapsed]
aws_instance.ec2_server: Creation complete after 42s [id=i-06ee72b4a7ea8256e]

Apply complete! Resources: 1 added, 0 changed, 0 destroyed.

Outputs:

ec2-server-ip-address = [
  "34.204.12.227",
]
[vcs@ terra]$
```

Figure 2-28. *Terraform apply output*

"Apply complete! Resources: 1 added, 0 changed, 0 destroyed." appears at the bottom of the screen.

Now you can navigate to AWS console (https://console.aws.amazon. com/ec2/v2/home), go to the appropriate region (as per our code), and review the resource created with the given name or as per the IP output from the server (see Figure 2-29).

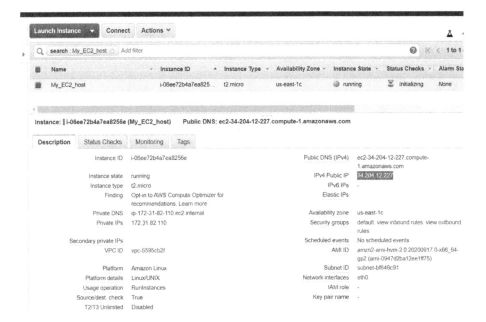

Figure 2-29. *Resource created from Terraform in AWS console*

Now that you have validated the outcome of the Terraform code, it's a good practice to delete that resource; otherwise, it costs if left running. For that, run the destroy command as follows to delete all the resources and their dependencies (see Figures 2-30 and 2-31).

```
terraform destroy
```

```
[vcs@ terra]$  terraform destroy
aws_instance.ec2_server: Refreshing state... [id=i-06ee72b4a7ea8256e]

An execution plan has been generated and is shown below.
Resource actions are indicated with the following symbols:
    destroy

Terraform will perform the following actions:

  # aws_instance.ec2_server will be destroyed
    resource "aws_instance" "ec2_server" {
        ami                          = "ami-0947d2ba12ee1ff75" -> null
        arn                          = "arn:aws:ec2:us-east-1:8 /8:instance/i-06ee72b4a7ea8256e"
        associate_public_ip_address  = true -> null
        availability_zone            = "us-east-1c" -> null
        cpu_core_count               = 1 -> null
        cpu_threads_per_core         = 1 -> null
        disable_api_termination      = false -> null
        ebs_optimized                = false -> null
        get_password_data            = false -> null
        hibernation                  = false -> null
        id                           = "i-06ee72b4a7ea8256e" -> null
        instance_state               = "running" -> null
        instance_type                = "t2.micro" -> null
        ipv6_address_count           = 0 -> null
        ipv6_addresses               = [] -> null
        monitoring                   = false -> null
        primary_network_interface_id = "eni-07caf4ebbd20a5198" -> null
        private_dns                  = "ip-172-31-82-110.ec2.internal" -> null
        private_ip                   = "172.31.82.110" -> null
        public_dns                   = "ec2-34-204-12-227.compute-1.amazonaws.com" -> null
        public_ip                    = "34.204.12.227" -> null
        secondary_private_ips        = [] -> null
        security_groups              = [
            "default",
        ] -> null
        source_dest_check            = true -> null
        subnet_id                    = "subnet-bf646c_1" -> null
        tags                         = {
            "Environment" = "MyDemo"
            "Name"        = "My_EC2_host"
        } -> null
```

Figure 2-30. *Terraform destroy*

```
Plan: 0 to add, 0 to change, 1 to destroy.

Changes to Outputs:
    ec2-server-ip-address = [
        "34.204.12.227",
    ] -> null

Do you really want to destroy all resources?
  Terraform will destroy all your managed infrastructure, as shown above.
  There is no undo. Only 'yes' will be accepted to confirm.

  Enter a value: yes

aws_instance.ec2_server: Destroying... [id=i-06ee72b4a7ea8256e]
aws_instance.ec2_server: Still destroying... [id=i-06ee72b4a7ea8256e, 10s elapsed]
aws_instance.ec2_server: Still destroying... [id=i-06ee72b4a7ea8256e, 20s elapsed]
aws_instance.ec2_server: Destruction complete after 30s

Destroy complete! Resources: 1 destroyed.
[vcs@ terra]$
```

Figure 2-31. *Terraform resource destroyed*

What's New in Terraform 0.14

This chapter worked with Terraform 0.13. Terraform upgrades are frequent, and every new version has enhanced features.

Terraform 0.14 is the latest version. The release and upgrade notes are at https://github.com/hashicorp/terraform/blob/v0.14/CHANGELOG.md.

Terraform 0.14 vs. Terraform 0.13

- Terraform 0.14 adds support to declare a variable as sensitive to prevent it from being visible to the naked eye.

- The init command creates a lock in the configuration directory, which can be checked into version control to ensure the same version of the plug-in is consumed in the next run.

- Terraform's latest version supports read and write of all compatible state files from a future version of Terraform.

Summary

This chapter covered Terraform's main concepts. We learned how to subscribe to Terraform Cloud, install Terraform CLI, and execute simple code to provision a service on AWS.

The next chapter covers Terraform programming constructs and looks at how they can be leveraged to write automation code.

CHAPTER 3

Understanding Terraform Programming Constructs

This chapter covers Terraform's programming components. Designing an infrastructure with Terraform code requires some basic understanding of the programming components. The following are the programming components covered in this chapter.

- HCL

- Resources

- Providers

- Input variables

- Output values

- Local values

- Modules

© Navin Sabharwal, Sarvesh Pandey and Piyush Pandey 2021
N. Sabharwal et al., *Infrastructure-as-Code Automation Using Terraform, Packer, Vault, Nomad and Consul*, https://doi.org/10.1007/978-1-4842-7129-2_3

- Data sources

- Backend configurations

- Provisioners

Configuration Language

Terraform uses its own configuration language, called HashiCorp Configuration Language, or HCL. It is a declarative language that lets you achieve your configuration goals without concern about the sequence of steps to do it. Terraform configuration consists of a root module, where evaluation begins, along with a tree of child modules created when one module calls another.

Arguments, Blocks, and Expressions

The terraform language syntax is build around below key constructs:

- **Blocks** are the containers where the configuration of a resource is kept. Blocks are comprised of block-types, labels, arguments and nested blocks (e.g., a dynamic block).

- **Arguments** assign a value to a specific name. They are assigned within blocks.

- **Expressions** are literal or referenced values for arguments.

- **Values** can be combined using built-in functions.

Now let's look at the code snippet shown in Listing 3-1. The block in the block-type resource acts as a container for the forwarding rule configuration. Multiple arguments (like project = var.project) are present, where the name is an expression and the referenced value is var.project. Similarly, for a load_balancing_scheme expression, there is a literal value called EXTERNAL.

Listing 3-1. Block Configuration

```
resource "google_compute_forwarding_rule" "default" {
  project               = var.project
  name                  = var.name
  target                = google_compute_target_pool.default.
                          self_link
  load_balancing_scheme = "EXTERNAL"
  port_range            = var.service_port
  region                = var.region
  ip_address            = var.ip_address
  ip_protocol           = var.ip_protocol
}
```

Code Organization

Terraform configuration files have a .tf extension. It supports JSON-based variants by using a .tf.json extension.

The basic Terraform configuration contains only a single .tf file. The configuration can be enhanced by adding more resources. This is done by creating new configuration files in the same root module or organizing them in child modules. A module can also be a combination of .tf and .tf. json, which can be managed together in a directory.

Configuration Ordering

Terraform is a declarative language and does not worry about the order of the resources. It maintains a dependency order relationship within the resources, maps them identically to real-world resources.

Resources

Resources are the major building blocks in Terraform, any infrastructure component(virtual machine, networks, databases etc.) in an environment which needs to be created and managed via terraform is depicted as a resource in configuration file. Let's review the code snippet shown in Listing 3-2. The resource block declares a resource-type (google compute disk) with a given local name (test-d01-data). The name refers to the resource from elsewhere in the same Terraform module, but has no significance outside that module's scope. The resource type and name together serve as an identifier for a given resource and must be unique within a module.

Within the block body (between { and }) are the configuration arguments for the resource. Most arguments in this section depend on the resource type, and in this example, type, size, and zone are arguments defined specifically for "google compute disk".

Listing 3-2. Resources Configuration

```
resource "google_compute_disk" "test-d01-data" {
  name  = "test-d01-data"
  type  = "pd-ssd"
  size  =  "10"
  zone  = "us-west1-a"
}
```

Provider

Provider is a Terraform plug-in that offers a collection of resource types. Each Provider plug-in offers a set of resource types and defines which arguments it accepts, which attributes it exports, and how changes to resources of that type are applied to remote APIs. Providers also offer local utilities for tasks, like generating random numbers for unique resource names.

Let's review the code snippet shown in Listing 3-3. The "google" provider specifies that the resources belong in the Google platform, whereas project and credentials are the components specifying the project and the credentials required to authorize the API.

Listing 3-3. Provider Configuration

```
   provider "google" {
 project     = "crafty-student-290205"
 credentials = file("crafty-student-290205-6d4ebc9cd946.json")
}
```

Before a new provider is added to a configuration, Terraform must install the provider. If a persistent working directory is used, run terraform init to install the provider. Once installed, the download resides in the current working directory. To make the provider global (i.e., out of the bounds of the working directory), you can enable a plug-in cache in the Terraform configuration file in the terraform.d directory, as shown in Listing 3-4. This directory must exist before Terraform cache plug-ins are enabled. Terraform cannot create this directory itself.

Listing 3-4. Plug-in Configuration

```
plugin_cache_dir   = "$HOME/.terraform.d/plugin-cache"
disable_checkpoint = true
```

Input Variables

Input variables are often called Terraform variables. They are used as parameters that allow certain resource values to be taken as either an input from a var file or during runtime. This allows the module to be customized without altering the module's source code. Now let's review the code snippet shown in Listing 3-5.

Listing 3-5. Input Variables

```
variable "disk-type" {
  type        = string
  default     = ""
  description = "Input from the user"
}

variable "zone" {
  type        = string
  default     = "us-east1-c"
  description = "Input from the user"
}

variable "size" {
  type        = number
  default     = ""
  description = "Input from the user"
}

variable "ami_id" {
  type = string

  validation {
    condition     = can(regex("^ami-", var.example))
    error_message = "Must be an AMI id, starting with \"ami-\"."
  }
}
```

The disk type, zone, and size of the Google compute disk are defined as variables to be taken as input from the user during runtime. A variable can also be initialized with a default value as specified for variable "zone" in the above Listing 3-5. This makes the code robust and provides flexibility. A description can be provided in the variable to make it more understandable.

The last example includes a validation block introduced in Terraform 0.13, where a condition (`can(regex("^ami-", var.example))`) is given to validate that the input must contain the ami prefix in the variable; otherwise, it generates an error message ("Must be an AMI id, starting with \"ami-" ").

The variable name (e.g., variable "size") assigns a value to a variable and must be unique among all the variables in the same module.

The name of a variable can be any valid identifier except the following.

- Source

- Version

- Providers

- Count

- for_each

- locals

- depends_on

- Lifecycle

Type constraints in variables are a mixture of type keywords and type constructors. The following are supported.

- String

- Number

- Boolean

Type constructors define complex keywords. The following are examples.

- list(<TYPE>)

- set(<TYPE>)

- map(<TYPE>)

- object({<ATTR NAME> = <TYPE>, ... })

- tuple([<TYPE>, ...])

If the variable type is unknown, or if you are unsure about the type, then the "any" keyword can be used, making any value acceptable.

Variables can also be passed as vars files during the `terraform plan` and `apply` phases. The following is an example.

```
terraform apply -var-file="testing.tfvars"
```

Environment Variables

An external environment variable can be exported in the current working shell. In Listing 3-6, TF_VAR_image_id is an external variable. This variable can be used in Terraform code without having to implicitly mention it. This value is used for AMI throughout the code without specifying it.

Listing 3-6. Environment Variables

```
export TF_VAR_image_id=ami-08bcc13ad2c143073
```

The precedence order of variables is as follows:

1. vars is passed at the command line (–var-file).

2. Terraform.tfvars.json is next in precedence.

3. Terraform.tfvars follows.

4. Environment variables have the least precedence.

Output Values

Output values correspond to the values returned by Terraform modules whenever `terraform apply` is run to apply a configuration. End users can query the output by running the `terraform output` command.

These variables come in handy in the following cases.

- A child module wants to send the data or its resource attributes to the parent module.

- External scripts want to query certain attributes from a Terraform module.

Resources created by Terraform have certain output values that can be later used by any other resource or by any processes.

Now let's review the code snippet shown in Listing 3-7. The output block is defined with block-type webserver_ip storing a compute instance's NIC IP.

Listing 3-7. Output Variables

```
output "webserver_ip" {
  value = google_compute_instance.default.network_
  interface.0.access_config.0.nat_ip
}
```

To access the output from Listing 3-7, you can traverse to location 'module.webserver.webserver_ip' wherein webserver corresponds to the block label name given to the resource "google_compute_instance".

Output blocks can optionally include arguments like description, sensitive, and depends_on.

- **Description** can be included in the output block to provide information about the output and its purpose, as shown in Listing 3-8.

Listing 3-8. Output Block

```
output "webserver_ip" {
  value = google_compute_instance.default.network_
  interface.0.access_config.0.nat_ip
  description = public ip of instance
}
```

- **Sensitive** is used when the output is confidential and not to be shown on the command line (e.g., passwords), as shown in Listing 3-9.

Listing 3-9. Output Block (Sensitive Data)

```
output "db_password" {
  value       = aws_db_instance.db.password
  description = "The password for logging in to the database."
  sensitive   = true
}
```

- **depends_on** is used when one of the resources depends on the value of the output result, as shown in Listing 3-10. It creates a relationship within the nodes with a dependency graph.

Listing 3-10. Depends_on Use Case

```
output "instance_ip_addr" {
  value       = aws_instance.server.private_ip
  description = "The private IP address of the main server
                instance."

  depends_on = [
    # Security group rule must be created before this IP
    address could
```

```
    # actually be used, otherwise the services will be
    unreachable.
    aws_security_group_rule.local_access
  ]
}
```

Here the resource instance_ip_addr needs to be created after fetching the value of aws_security_group_rule.local_access. A depends_on output must always have a description to make it easier for the future maintainer of the code.

Local Values

Local values in Terraform represent certain expressions or variables in the file whose values are constant and are invoked at multiple places in the code. For example, using locals for the bucket name in different cloud providers is a good idea because it creates randomness in the name.

Now let's review the code snippet shown in Listing 3-11. The two locals—is_postgres and is_mysql—are defined inside a block called locals. These values are available throughout the code.

Listing 3-11. Defining Locals

```
locals {
  # Determine the engine type
  is_postgres = replace(var.engine, "POSTGRES", "") != var.
  engine
  is_mysql    = replace(var.engine, "MYSQL", "") != var.engine
}
```

A local value can be used anywhere in the code. The value is called by local.<Name>, as shown in Listing 3-12.

Listing 3-12. Using Local Values

```
resource "google_sql_user" "default" {
  depends_on = [google_sql_database.default]

  project  = var.project
  name     = var.master_user_name
  instance = google_sql_database_instance.master.name
  host     = local.is_postgres ? null : var.master_user_host
  password = var.master_user_password
}
```

Here the host expression gets its value by fetching and comparing the value of the local is_postgres. The expression determines the value from the local is_postgres and puts it in the conditional logic.

Local values help remove duplicate calls in configuration files. Local values are analogous to local variables in programming languages.

Modules

A module is a container in which all the resources are defined to be used together. Every Terraform code has one essential module, called a *root module*, which contains all the resources in the .tf configuration file. A module can call other modules, which allows inclusion of the child module's resources concisely into the configuration. Modules can be called multiple times, either within the same configuration or in separate configurations, making the code reusable.

Calling a module with an expression means to include the contents of the module in the configuration file along with relevant input variables.

Now let's review the code snippet shown in Listing 3-13.

Listing 3-13. Module Configuration

```
module "load_balancer" {
  source       = "GoogleCloudPlatform/lb/google"
  version      = "~> 2.0.0"
  region       = var.region
  name         = "load-balancer"
  service_port = 80
  target_tags  = ["allow-lb-service"]
  network      = var.network
}
```

In listing 3-13 the source argument is calling the GoogleCloudPlatform/lb/google module.

For all modules, a source argument is a mandate that is specified while invoking a module in the code. This location can be a local directory or a remote module source containing configuration files related to the module.

After the addition, removal, or modification of a module, Terraform needs to be synchronized with the new module by running a terraform init command. By default, terraform init does not upgrade an installed module. Upgrade of an installed module can be initiated by using the -upgrade flag.

Calling a module via terraform configuration does not implies that attributes of the resources can be accessed directly as the resources are encapsulated. To get the output values, certain selective values need to be exported from it.

Now let's review the code snippet shown in Listing 3-14. Instead of calling the complete module, the value of default.ip_address is selected and displayed as an output.

Listing 3-14. Module Output

```
output "external_ip" {
  description = "The external ip address of the forwarding rule."
  value       = google_compute_forwarding_rule.default.ip_address
}
```

Terraform code is confined within a working directory; if the working directory is changed, Terraform takes it as a new location with added resources. The `terraform state mv` command is used to transfer resource states into modules.

Creating a Custom Module

Terraform treats any local directory referenced in a module block's source argument as a module. A typical file structure for a new module is shown in Figure 3-1.

```
custom-module/
├── LICENSE
├── main.tf
├── outputs.tf
├── README.md
└── variables.tf
```

Figure 3-1. *Directory structure*

You can create a module with a single .tf file or use any other file structure you like. Typically, each of the files shown in Figure 3-1 serves a specific purpose.

- LICENSE contains the license under which your module is distributed. When you share your module, the LICENSE file let users know the terms of usage.

- README.md contains documentation describing how to utilize the module in markdown format. Terraform does not use this file, but services like Terraform Registry and GitHub display the contents of this file to people who visit the module's Terraform Registry or GitHub page.

- main.tf contains the main set of configurations for your module. You can also create other configuration files and organize them however it makes sense for the project.

- variables.tf contains the variable definitions for the module. When the module is invoked in the configuration file, the variables are configured as arguments in the module block. Since all Terraform values must be defined, any variables that are not given a default value become required arguments. Variables with default values can also be provided as module arguments, overriding the default value.

- outputs.tf contains the output definitions for the module, which you can use to extract internal information about the state of the resources.

Now let's create a module for the s3 bucket in main.tf, as shown in Listing 3-15.

Listing 3-15. Creating a Custom Module

```
# Terraform configuration

resource "aws_s3_bucket" "s3_bucket" {
  bucket = var.bucket_name
  acl    = "public-read"
  policy = <<EOF
{
    "Version": "2012-10-17",
    "Statement": [
        {
            "Sid": "PublicReadGetObject",
            "Effect": "Allow",
            "Principal": "*",
            "Action": [
                "s3:GetObject"
            ],
            "Resource": [
                "arn:aws:s3:::${var.bucket_name}/*"
            ]
        }
    ]
}
EOF

  website {
    index_document = "index.html"
    error_document = "error.html"
  }

  tags = var.tags
}
```

The variables are defined in Listing 3-16.

Listing 3-16. Defining Custom Module Variables

```
variable "bucket_name" {
  description = "Name of the s3 bucket. Must be unique."
  type = string
}

variable "tags" {
  description = "Tags to set on the bucket."
  type = map(string)
  default = {}
}
```

The output is defined in Listing 3-17.

Listing 3-17. Module Output

```
# Output variable definitions

output "arn" {
  description = "ARN of the bucket"
  value       = aws_s3_bucket.s3_bucket.arn
}

output "name" {
  description = "Name (id) of the bucket"
  value       = aws_s3_bucket.s3_bucket.id
}

output "website_endpoint" {
  description = "Domain name of the bucket"
  value       = aws_s3_bucket.s3_bucket.website_endpoint
}
```

Whenever you add a new module to a configuration, Terraform must install it before it can be used. Both the `terraform get` and `terraform init` commands install and update modules. The `terraform init` command also initializes backends and installs plug-ins.

Now let's install the module by running `terraform get`, and write the configuration in the main.tf file, as shown in Listing 3-18.

Listing 3-18. Installing Module

```
module "website_s3_bucket" {
  source = "./modules/aws-s3-static-website-bucket"

  bucket_name = "<UNIQUE BUCKET NAME>"

  tags = {
    Terraform   = "true"
    Environment = "dev"
  }
}
```

Execute the `terraform apply` command to provision the bucket using a custom module, as shown in Listing 3-19. In the configuration files, make sre you have added the AWS account information created in Chapter 2.

Listing 3-19. Terraform Apply with Module

```
$ terraform apply
An execution plan has been generated and is shown below.
Resource actions are indicated with the following symbols:
  + create
```

Terraform will perform the following actions:

...

```
  # module.website_s3_bucket.aws_s3_bucket.s3_bucket will be
    created
  + resource "aws_s3_bucket" "s3_bucket" {
      + acceleration_status        = (known after apply)
```

...

Do you want to perform these actions?
  Terraform will perform the actions described above.
  Only 'yes' will be accepted to approve.

  Enter a value:

Meta-arguments like version, count, provider, and depends_on are used when creating code. Each has special relevance to usage in the module.

Version

A version constraint string specifies acceptable versions of the module, as shown in Listing 3-20.

Listing 3-20. Meta-Argument Version

```
module "ssm" {
  source  = "./aws"
  version = "0.2"
}
```

Here, version 0.2 is passed as a value to fetch the values from the ./aws source inside the ssm module.

The version attribute accepts a string value. Terraform tries to install the version of the module in the attribute value. The version attribute is only applicable for modules published in the Terraform module registry or Terraform Cloud private module registry.

Modules residing in other sources may have their own version-control mechanism, which can be specified in the source string. Modules residing in local directories do not support versions; since they are loaded from the same source repository, they always share the same version as their caller.

count and for_each

count and for_each create multiple instances of the same resource, as shown in Listing 3-21. These arguments have the same syntax and type constraints as for_each and count when used with resources.

Listing 3-21. For_each Example

```
Resource "aws_iam" "example" { {
  for_each = toset(var.user_names)
  source   = "./aws/iam"
  name     = each.value
}
```

The for_each constraint creates an IAM user matching the set user_names defined in the /aws/iam module. The /aws/iam child module has a configuration to create IAM users. for_each creates multiple users with a special key name: each.value. Resources from child modules are prefixed with module.module_name[module index] when displayed in the UI. In our example, the ./aws/iam module contains aws_iam_user.example. The two instances of this module produce IAM user resources with `module.iam["ram"].aws_iam_user.example` and `module.iam["rambo"].aws_iam_user.example` resource addresses. The `ram` and `rambo` values are taken as variables.

depends_on Module

In previous versions of Terraform, module instances served only as separate namespaces. They were not nodes in Terraform's dependency graphs. Terraform has always tracked dependencies via the input variables and output values of a module. But users have frequently requested a concise way to declare that all objects inside a module share a particular dependency in the calling module. Terraform v0.13 introduces this capability by allowing depends_on as a meta-argument inside module blocks, as shown in Listing 3-22.

Listing 3-22. Depends_on with Module

```
resource "aws_iam_policy_attachment" "example" {
  name       = "example"
  roles      = [aws_iam_role.example.name]
  policy_arn = aws_iam_policy.example.arn
}

module "uses-role" {
  # ...

  depends_on = [aws_iam_policy_attachment.example]
}
```

Providers

Provider in Terraform acts as a plug-in to integrate with third-party systems. Each invoked provider brings a set of resource types or data sources that Terraform can manage. Provider configurations can be defined only in a root Terraform module.

Once changes are applied, Terraform retains a reference to the provider configuration that was most recently used to create the resources in its state file. This is why `terraform plan` contains resources that have references to the old configuration if the provider starts to fail. To solve this problem, Terraform provider needs to be reintroduced in the configuration file.

Provider Version Constraints in Modules

Although provider *configurations* are shared between modules, each module must declare its own provider requirements so that Terraform can ensure that there is a single version of the provider that is compatible with all modules in the configuration and to specify the source address that serves as the global (module-agnostic) identifier for a provider.

Now let's look at the provider shown in Figure 3-2.

```
provider "vsphere" {
  user            = "xxxxxxxxx"
  password        = "xxxxxxxxx"
  vsphere_server  = "xxxxxxxxx"        You, seconds ago • Uncommitted changes
  version         = "1.24.2"
  # If you have a self-signed cert
  allow_unverified_ssl = true
}
```

Figure 3-2. *Provider versions*

Here the module version required for the vSphere provider is 1.24.2. A Terraform configuration file can have multiple provider configurations, such as one for GCP and another for AWS or different versions of the same cloud.

Automatic Installation of Third-Party Providers

Terraform v0.13 introduced a new hierarchical provider-naming scheme that allows HashiCorp providers to occupy namespaces separate from providers developed or distributed by others. Third-party providers are indexed in Terraform Registry and automatically installed by Terraform.

The new provider naming scheme includes a registry hostname and a namespace in addition to the provider name. The existing AzureRM provider is now known as hashicorp/azurerm, which is short for registry. terraform.io/hashicorp/azurerm. Providers not developed by HashiCorp can be selected from their own namespaces, using a new provider requirements syntax added in Terraform v0.13.

Let's review the code snippet shown in Listing 3-23.

Listing 3-23. Third-Party Providers

```
terraform {
  required_providers {
    jetstream = {
      source  = "nats-io/jetstream"
      version = "0.0.5"
    }
  }
}
```

The nats-io/jetstream address is short for registry.terraform.io/nats-io/jetstream, indicating a third-party provider published in the public Terraform registry for widespread use.

The provider registry protocol is eventually published so that others can implement it, in which case other hostnames become usable in source addresses. At the time of writing this guide, only the public Terraform Registry at registry.terraform.io was available for general testing.

As a measure of backward compatibility for commonly used existing providers, Terraform 0.13 includes a special case that if no explicit source is selected for a provider, Terraform creates one by selecting registry. terraform.io as the origin registry and "hashicorp" as the namespace.

For example, if "aws" provider is invoked in the configuration file without the required_providers argument, terraform assumes the value hashicorp/aws which is short for registry.terraform.io/hashicorp/aws.

Provider Plug-ins in a Local Filesystem

While `terraform init` supports the automatic installation of HashiCorp distributed providers, third-party-packaged providers must be installed manually in a local filesystem. Some users also chose to create local copies of the HashiCorp-distributed providers to avoid repeatedly re-downloading them.

Terraform v0.13 still supports local copies of providers—officially called *local mirrors*. But the new multi-level addressing scheme for providers means that the expected directory structure in these local directories has changed to include each provider's origin registry hostname and namespace, giving a directory structure like the following.

```
"registry.terraform.io/hashicorp/azurerm/2.0.0/linux_amd64/
terraform-provider-azurerm_v2.0.0"
```

In this example, terraform-provider-azurerm_v2.0.0 is an executable residing inside the provider's distribution zip file. The containing directory structure allows Terraform to understand that this is a plug-in intended to serve the hashicorp/azurerm (short for registry.terraform.io/hashicorp/azurerm) provider at version 2.0.0 on the platform linux_amd64.

If you use local copies of providers that `terraform init` would normally be able to autoinstall, you can use the new Terraform `providers` mirror command to automatically construct the directory structure for the providers in the current configuration.

```
terraform providers mirror ~/.terraform.d/plugins
```

This creates local mirrors in one of the directories Terraform consults by default on non-Windows systems. This same directory structure is used for all the directories in which Terraform searches for plug-ins.

Note that due to the directory structure being multi-level, Terraform no longer looks for provider plug-ins in the same directory where the Terraform executable is installed. It is not conventional for there to be subdirectories under directories, like /usr/bin on a Unix system.

Data Sources

Data sources allow a Terraform configuration to use information defined outside Terraform or defined by a different Terraform configuration (e.g., getting the details of an Amazon VPC defined manually or outside the Terraform configuration file). A data source is accessed via a special kind of resource known as a *data resource*, declared using the data block shown in Listing 3-24.

Listing 3-24. Data Sources

```
data "aws_ami" "std_ami" {
  most_recent = true
  owners      = ["amazon"]

filter {
    name   = "root-device-type"
    values = ["ebs"]
  }
```

```
filter {
    name    = "virtualization-type"
    values = ["hvm"]
  }
}

resource "aws_instance" "myec2" {
  ami             = data.aws_ami.std_ami.id
  instance_type = "t2.micro"
}
```

The data block requests that Terraform read from a given data source. In this case, the AMI details are read from the available ones on the aws_ ami resource, with a reference pointer called std_ami, through which it is called inside the configuration.

The data source and name together serve as an identifier for a given resource and must be unique within a module.

Within the block body (between { and }) are query constraints defined by the data source. root-device-type and virtualization-type are the query constraints with the filtered values. They are different from managed resources (defined with resource block) so that data resources can only perform read operations for the resource, whereas managed resources perform all CRUD operations.

Each data resource is associated with a single data source, specifying the kind of object it reads.

Most of the data source arguments specified within data blocks are specific to the selected data source. These arguments can make full use of expressions and other dynamic HCL features. However, there are some meta-arguments that are defined by Terraform and apply across all data sources.

Backend Configuration

The *backend* in Terraform determines how the state is loaded and how an operation such as `apply` is executed. This abstraction enables non-local file state storage and remote execution. The most common way to configure the backend is to be on a remote site, making it possible for multiple users to work on the same code. The following are the key benefits of using the backend.

- **Team collaboration:** Since backends are managed on a remote site, multiple users can work on it, which reduces time and effort. Locks are used for preventing corruption, and versioning is enabled to keep multiple copies of a code, maintaining a which tracks progress for everyone.

- **Preventing sensitive data exposure:** State is retrieved from the backends on demand and is only stored in memory. If a backend such as Amazon S3 is used, then the only location the state ever is persisted is in S3. There is no risk of sensitive data being exposed.

- **Remote operations:** In a large infrastructure, `terraform apply` can take a long time, so Terraform supports remote operations, making the code run on its own. With locking, different environments can be maintained at the backend.

Backends are configured with a nested backend block within the top-level Terraform block, as shown in Listing 3-25.

Listing 3-25. Backend Configuration

```
terraform {
  backend "s3" {
    bucket = "backend_bucket"
    key     = "./key"
    region = "us-east-1"
  }
}
```

Here S3 object storage is leveraged as a backend provider for the state file. Note that there can only be one backend per configuration, and the backend block cannot refer to named values like input variables, locals, or data source attributes.

Backend Types

Backend types are usually grouped into two categories.

- **Standard**: State management and functionalities in state storage and locking. Examples of a standard backend include S3 bucket, Consul, Azure RM, etcd, Manta, Kubernetes, and GCS.

- **Enhanced**: Everything in Standard plus remote operations. Examples of an enhanced backend are local and remote.

By default, Terraform does not have any backend. It uses the current working directory as the local backend for storing state files in a simple format.

The local backend stores the state on the local filesystem, locks that state using system APIs, and performs operations locally. This is the default backend.

The remote backend stores the Terraform state and may run operations in Terraform Cloud. When using full remote operations, `terraform plan` or terraform apply can be executed in Terraform Cloud's run environment, with log output streaming to the local terminal. Remote plan and apply use variable values from the associated Terraform Cloud workspace. Terraform Cloud can also be used with local operations, in which case the only state is stored in the Terraform Cloud backend.

The arguments used in the block's body are specific to the chosen backend type; they configure where and how the backend stores the configuration's state, and in some cases, configures other behavior.

Backend Initialization

Whenever a configuration's backend changes, `terraform init` must run again to validate and configure the backend before you can perform any plan, apply, or state operations. A simple copy/paste of the .tfstate file can also be done, but a backup should be created to manage any adverse situations.

Provisioners

Provisioners can model specific actions on the machine to prepare servers or other infrastructure objects for service.

Post-provisioning tasks, which can include agent onboarding, joining a domain, running hardening scripts, installing third-party clients for backup, antivirus, and so forth, can be achieved via provisioners.

Provisioners interact with remote servers over SSH (for Linux systems) or WinRM (for Windows). Provisioners run the scripts defined within the configuration on the servers by taking the session for servers and passing the script to the server, which is then available at the system booting stage.

This mechanism is analogous to a user data construct in other public cloud platforms.

Now let's review the code snippet shown in Listing 3-26. The local-exec provisioner requires no other configuration, but most other provisioners must connect to the remote system using SSH or WinRM. A connection block must be included so that Terraform knows how to communicate with the server.

Listing 3-26. Provisioners Use Case

```
resource "aws_instance" "web" {
  # ...

  provisioner "local-exec" {
    command = "echo The server's IP address is
    ${self.private_ip}"
  }
}
```

Creation-Time Provisioners

There are certain activities in which some action must be done on the resource while it is being created, such as booting a server in a bootstrapping sequence. These activities are only needed during the creation of the server and do not require a rollback at any other lifecycle state. In these cases, creation-time provisioners are used.

Creation-time provisioners are only run during creation, not during updating or any other lifecycle. They are meant to perform bootstrapping on a system.

When an error is encountered during the execution of a provisioner, the resource state is marked as tainted. Terraform plans the destroy and re-creates the resource on the next `terraform apply`. This is necessary because a failed provisioner means that all desired/required tasks specified within the provisioners did not run, leaving the final state of the resource different from what it should be.

Destroy-Time Provisioners

Provisioners specified with a when = destroy condition in the provisioner code lock are called *destory-time provisioners*. These provisioners are called before the resource is destroyed in Terraform. Listing 3-27 is an example of an aws_instance resource named web, and a provisioner is called at the destroy state.

Listing 3-27. Destroy Time Provisioners

```
resource "aws_instance" "web" {
  # ...

  provisioner "local-exec" {
    when    = destroy
    command = "echo 'Destroy-time provisioner'"
  }
}
```

The fail behavior for the destroy provisioners is similar to create-time provisioners (i.e., terraform will error and rerun the provisioners on the next terraform apply). Due to this behavior, care should be taken with destroy provisioners to be safe enough to run multiple times.

Destroy-time provisioners can only run if they remain in the configuration at the time a resource is destroyed. If a resource block with a destroy-time provisioner is removed entirely from the configuration, its provisioner configurations are removed along with it, and thus the destroy provisioner cannot run. You can use the following workaround to overcome this issue.

1. Update the resource configuration to include count = 0.

2. Apply the configuration to destroy any existing resource instances, including running the destroy provisioner.

3. Remove the resource block entirely from configuration, along with its provisioner blocks.

4. Apply again, at which point no further action should be taken since the resources were already destroyed.

A destroy-time provisioner within a resource that is tainted cannot run. This includes resources that are marked tainted from a failed creation-time provisioner or tainted manually using `terraform taint`.

Multiple Provisioners

In some scenarios, multiple actions need to be executed on the resource. In such cases, multiple provisioners can be specified in a single resource code (as shown in Listing 3-28).

Multiple provisioners are executed in the order they are defined in the configuration file. Only the provisioners that are valid for a given operation are run. The valid provisioners are run in the order they are defined in the configuration file.

Listing 3-28. Multiple Provisioners

```
resource "aws_instance" "web" {
  # ...

  provisioner "local-exec" {
    command = "echo first"
  }
```

```
provisioner "local-exec" {
  command = "echo second"
  }
}
```

Types of Provisioners

There are two prominent types of provisioners: generic and vendor.

Generic Provisioners

Generic provisioners are built-in provisioners provided by Terraform. They include file, local-exec, and remote-exec.

File Provisioners

File provisioners copy files from the machine executing Terraform to the newly created resource. A file provisioner supports both SSH and WinRM type connections, as shown in Listing 3-29.

Listing 3-29. File Provisioner

```
provisioner "file" {
    source      = "/etc/demo.txt"
    destination = "/usr/demo.txt"
  }
```

The file provisioner copies the contents of the /etc/demo.txt directory to the /use/demo.txt destination inside the Terraform configuration file.

Note A file provisioner can upload a complete directory to a remote machine. Make sure the destination directory already exists. Use a remote-exec provisioner before the file provisioner to create the directory if you need to. If you use the winrm connection type, the destination directory is created if it does not already exist.

Local-Exec Provisioners

The local-exec provisioner invokes a local executable after a resource is created, as shown in Listing 3-30. This process is on the machine running Terraform, not on the resource, and there is no guarantee that it is in an operable state.

Listing 3-30. Local Exec Provisioner

```
resource "vsphere_virtual_machine" "tfe-resource2" {
  name             = "XXXXXXXX"
  ## resource code
 provisioner "local-exec" {
command = "echo ${data.vsphere_datastore.datastore.d} >>
datastoreid.txt"
}
}
```

Interpreters can be specified for a command to be executed with Terraform, as shown in Listing 3-31.

Listing 3-31. Local-exec with Interpreter

```
resource "null_resource" "example" {
  provisioner "local-exec" {
    command = "Get-Process > getprocess.txt"
    interpreter = ["PowerShell", "-Command"]
  }
}
```

Remote-Exec Provisioners

The remote-exec provisioner invokes a script on a remote resource after it is created, as shown in Listing 3-32. It can be used to run a configuration management tool, bootstrap into a cluster, and so forth. The remote-exec provisioner supports both SSH and WinRM type connections.

Listing 3-32. Remote-exec Provisioner

```
  provisioner "remote-exec" {
    inline = [
      hostnamectl set-hostname test
    ]
  }
}
```

Vendor Provisioners

Vendor provisioners allow third-party software vendors to configure and run the respective client on remote machines. Examples of vendor provisioners include chef, habitat, puppet, and salt-masterless provisioners.

Chef Provisioners

The chef provisioner, supported by SSH and WinRM connections, is responsible for installing and configuring the chef client on a remote resource. To use a specific type chef of provisioner, there are a few prerequisites that must be fulfilled. Listing 3-33 is a sample chef provisioner configuration.

Listing 3-33. Chef Provisioner

```
resource "aws_instance" "webmachine" {
  # ...

  provisioner "chef" {
    attributes_json = <<EOF
      {
        "key": "value",
        "app": {
          "cluster1": {
            "nodes": [
              "webserver1",
              "webserver2"
            ]
          }
        }
      }
    EOF

    environment     = "_default"
    client_options  = ["chef_license 'accept'"]
    run_list        = ["cookbook::recipe"]
    node_name       = "webserver1"
    secret_key      = "${file("../encrypted_data_bag_secret")}"
```

```
    server_url       = "https://chef.company.com/organizations/
                       org1"
    recreate_client = true
    user_name        = "bork"
    user_key         = "${file("../bork.pem")}"
    version          = "15.10.13"
    # If you have a self signed cert on your chef server change
    this to :verify_none
    ssl_verify_mode = ":verify_peer"
  }
}
```

Summary

This chapter covered the main concepts of HCL, Terraform's programming language. We learned how to leverage it while composing automation code.

The next chapter includes hands-on exercises using Terraform CLI to automate service provisioning on a public cloud like GCP and Azure.

CHAPTER 4

Automating Public Cloud Services Using Terraform

Previous chapters discussed using Terraform to automate AWS service provisioning using Terraform. This chapter uses hands-on exercises for automating Azure and GCP cloud services through Terraform. The following are the key topics covered in this chapter.

- Automating the GCP public cloud using Terraform
- Automating the Azure public cloud using Terraform

Automating the GCP Public Cloud Using Terraform

Before starting with Google Cloud Platform (GCP) automation using Terraform, we need to create a GCP account. The following explains how to create a GCP account and the service account used to integrate Terraform with GCP.

© Navin Sabharwal, Sarvesh Pandey and Piyush Pandey 2021
N. Sabharwal et al., *Infrastructure-as-Code Automation Using Terraform, Packer, Vault, Nomad and Consul*, https://doi.org/10.1007/978-1-4842-7129-2_4

The primary prerequisite for signing up with the platform is a Google account or any account configured with GSuite (now known as Google Workspace). GCP uses Google accounts for access management and authentication.

Note   If the account is already signed in, you are directly redirected to the GCP cloud console.

Enter **https://cloud.google.com** in the browser and create a Google Cloud account with your Google account (see Figure 4-1).

Figure 4-1. *Google Cloud Platform*

If you are eligible for the free tier, you are prompted for your account information (see Figure 4-2).

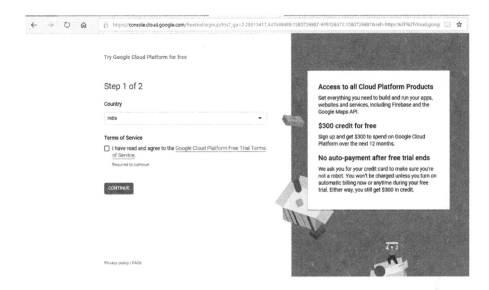

Figure 4-2. *GCP free tier registration step 1*

Select your country, agree to the Terms of Service and click on the Agree and Continue button. This takes you to the next step (see Figure 4-3), where you create and select your payment profile. Provide the required billing information however auto-debit does not happen unless you manually upgrade it (see Figure 4-3).

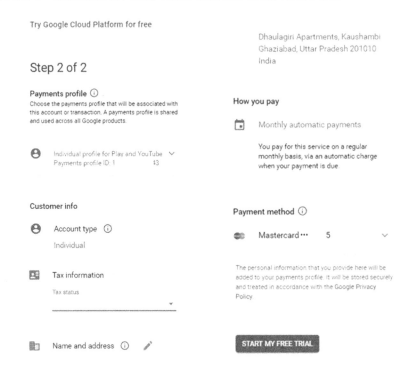

Figure 4-3. *GCP free tier registration step 2*

Google offers a free trial (worth $300) to everyone. It can be spent over 12 months, which is sufficient to explore all the exercises in the book and evaluate GCP further. Once you have specified all the details, click the Start My Free Trial button.

It takes a while for the registration to complete. Once the necessary validations are done, you are redirected to the Google console, and you are ready to start.

Now let's create the project for this exercise. A project is essentially a container for regrouping all IT and non-IT resources connected to a specific cloud project. Every project is identified by a specific parameter (see Table 4-1).

Table 4-1. *Project Parameters*

Parameter	Description
Name	Identifies and describes a project. The name is only for user reference and can be changed at any stage. The free tier allows you to create 24 projects.
Project ID	A unique string for identifying the project globally. It is created starting with the project name. Project ID is editable and can be changed. To create a project ID, you can use any lowercase letter, number, and hyphens. The only requirement is the uniqueness of the name. After this is entered, it is no longer possible to change it.
Project Number	A parameter that is autogenerated by GCP. You cannot manage or change this number.

To create a new project, click the Create a New Project as shown in Figure 4-4.

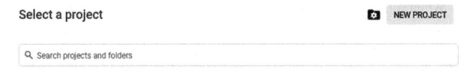

Figure 4-4. *New Project screen*

On the Select Organization drop-down list at the top of the page, select the organization that you want to create a project in. If you are a free trial user, skip this step because this list does not appear. Click Create Project.

In the New Project window, enter a project name and select an applicable account (see Figure 4-5).

Google Cloud Platform

New Project

Project name *
My Project 99157   ❓

Project ID: basic-formula-267506. It cannot be changed later.   EDIT

Location *
🏢 No organisation   BROWSE

Parent organisation or folder

CREATE   CANCEL

Figure 4-5. *New Project*

Remember the project ID, a unique name across all Google Cloud projects. It is referred to later as PROJECT_ID.

When you've finished entering your new project information, click Create. New Project is selected and appears as shown in Figure 4-6.

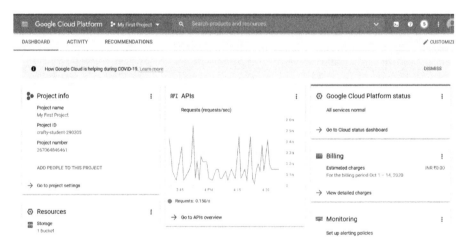

Figure 4-6. *New Project view*

To have programmatic access for Terraform to access GCP services, a service account must be created. This service account provides a credentials file which will be used in a Terraform configuration file to authorize access to the GCP environment. The following steps explain how to create a service account.

Navigate to the IAM service from Home (see Figure 4-7) and click the Service Accounts option.

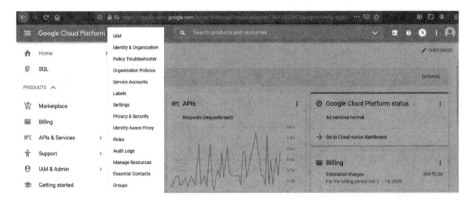

Figure 4-7. *Navigating through dashboard to IAM*

Click the +Create Service Account button to create a service account, as shown in Figure 4-8.

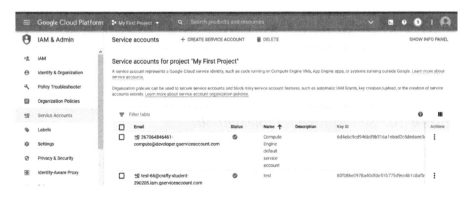

Figure 4-8. *Create service account*

Provide a name and description and click the Create button, as shown in Figure 4-9.

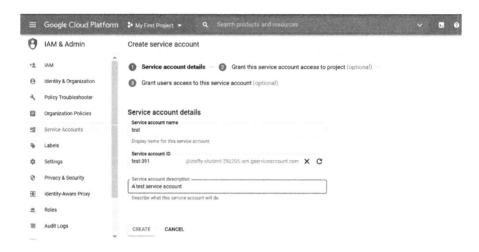

Figure 4-9. *Service account Name details*

In the Roles tab, select Project Editor, as shown in Figure 4-10.

Figure 4-10. *Service account role mapping*

Navigate to the Keys section and click the Add Key button to create a key (see Figure 4-11).

Figure 4-11. *Service account key*

Download and save the credentials file in a .json or .p12 format. This credentials file will be used to integrate Terraform with GCP.

In previous chapter we had installed Terraform. Now let's begin by creating GCP services using Terraform. Figure 4-12 shows an architecture diagram of the services provisioned using Terraform. The basic infrastructure consists of a VPC, a subnet, an instance, and GCS.

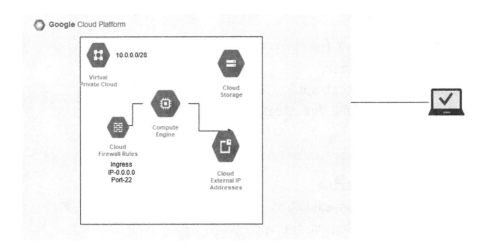

Figure 4-12. *Lab use-case architecture*

Creating a VPC and Subnet with Terraform

Clone the files from the GitHub repository used in this exercise by using the following command.

git clone https://github.com/dryice-devops/Terraform-GCP-UseCase-Automation

We used a Google provider and the service account credentials created in the previous section (see Listing 4-1).

Listing 4-1. Provider.tf

```
variable "project" {
  type        = string
  default     = "your project id"
  description = "GCP Project to be used for creating resources"
}
```

Listing 4-2 creates the VPC with "test-vpc" as the name and a subnet called "test". The variables are defined in vars.tf.

Listing 4-2. Vars.tf

```
variable "vpc_name" {
  type        = string
  default     = "test-vpc"
  description = "VPC for creating resources"
}
variable "region" {
  type        = string
  default     = "us-east1"
  description = "Region for vpc"
}
```

```
variable "subnet_name" {
  type        = string
  default     = "test"
  description = "Name of the Subnet to be Created"
}
```

Listing 4-3 shows the content of main.tf, which contains the logical code to create the network and subnetwork.

Listing 4-3. Main.tf

```
provider "google" {
  project     = var.project
  credentials = file("##############.json") // your
credentials.json file

#----------------------------------------------------------------
# Creating the VPC
#----------------------------------------------------------------

resource "google_compute_network" "vpc" {
 name                      = var.vpc_name
 auto_create_subnetworks = "false"
}

#----------------------------------------------------------------
# Creating the Subnet
#----------------------------------------------------------------

resource "google_compute_subnetwork" "subnet" {
 name          = var.subnet_name
 ip_cidr_range = "10.2.0.0/16"
 network       = var.vpc_name
 depends_on    = ["google_compute_network.vpc"]
 region        = var.region
}
```

This example creates a VPC and a subnet that keeps the subnet's autocreation as false. test-vpc has a subnet called test-subnet, in which the dependency on the VPC is mentioned by depends_on.

The name of the VPC network and subnetwork are displayed on the output screen with the help of the output.tf file (see Listing 4-4).

Listing 4-4. Output.tf

```
output "network_name" {
  value       = google_compute_network.vpc.name
  description = "The name of the VPC being created"
}

output "subnets" {
  value       = google_compute_subnetwork.subnet.name
  description = "The created subnet resources"
}
```

Run terraform init as shown in Figure 4-13. It is a good practice to run terraform plan before running terraform apply because it provides a skeleton view of what is to be created and how they are dependent on each other.

```
[avinaw.sharma@dryicelabs.com@mycloud0215 compute]$ terraform init

Initializing the backend...

Initializing provider plugins...

The following providers do not have any version constraints in configuration,
so the latest version was installed.

To prevent automatic upgrades to new major versions that may contain breaking
changes, it is recommended to add version = "..." constraints to the
corresponding provider blocks in configuration, with the constraint strings
suggested below.

* provider.google: version = "~> 3.40"

Terraform has been successfully initialized!

You may now begin working with Terraform. Try running "terraform plan" to see
any changes that are required for your infrastructure. All Terraform commands
should now work.

If you ever set or change modules or backend configuration for Terraform,
rerun this command to reinitialize your working directory. If you forget, other
commands will detect it and remind you to do so if necessary.
```

Figure 4-13. *GCP Terraform code init*

Creating a Virtual Machine with Terraform

The configuration in Listing 4-5 creates an instance using the Google compute engine service. To create a compute engine, you need to mention the parameters shown in vars.tf. In GCP, passing the SSH keys is not passed like the other cloud providers; instead, it is passed as metadata. Also, the firewall rules are attached to the compute engine through tags. Finally, the web server IP is fetched as the output value. Make sure that you use a different directory for each GCP service to avoid any errors while running terraform init, plan, and apply.

Listing 4-5. Vars.tf

```
variable "machine-type" {
  type        = string
  default     = "n1-standard-1"
  description = "Disk to be snapshotted"
}

variable "zone" {
  type        = string
  default     = "us-east1-c"
  description = "Input from the user"
}

variable "region" {
  type        = string
  default     = "us-east1"
  description = "Input from the user"
}
```

```
variable "image" {
  type        = string
  default     = "centos-7-v20200910"
  description = "Input from the user"
}
```

The main.tf file contains the operational logic to create the compute engine and firewall rule to connect the virtual machine, as shown in Listing 4-6.

Listing 4-6. Main.tf

```
provider "google" {
  project     = var.project
  credentials = file("###############.json") // credentials.
  json to be used here
}

resource "google_compute_instance" "default" {
  name            = "test"
  machine_type = var.machine-type
  zone            = var.zone
  allow_stopping_for_update = true

  tags = ["ssh"]

labels = {
    environment = "test"
    project = "test"
  }
```

```
  boot_disk {
    initialize_params {
      image = var.image
    }
  }

  network_interface {
    network = "default"

    access_config {
        // Ephemeral IP
    }

  }

  metadata = {
    ssh-keys = "your ssh keys to login"
  }
}
# allow ssh traffic
resource "google_compute_firewall" "allow-ssh" {
  name = "allow-ssh"
  network = "default"
  allow {
    protocol = "tcp"
    ports    = ["22"]
  }
 source_ranges = ["0.0.0.0/0"]
 target_tags = ["ssh"]
}
```

The compute engine public IP is displayed on the output screen with the help of the output.tf file (see Listing 4-7).

Listing 4-7. Output.tf

```
output "webserver_ip" {
  value = google_compute_instance.default.network_
  interface.0.access_config.0.nat_ip
}
```

Now run `terraform init`, `plan`, and `apply`, as shown in Figure 4-14. The output is shown in Figure 4-15.

Figure 4-14. *GCP Terraform code plan*

```
Do you want to perform these actions?
  Terraform will perform the actions described above.
  Only 'yes' will be accepted to approve.

  Enter a value: yes

google_compute_instance.default: Creating...
google_compute_instance.default: Still creating... [10s elapsed]
google_compute_instance.default: Creation complete after 18s [id=projects/crafty-student-290205/zones/us-east1-c/instances/test]

Apply complete! Resources: 1 added, 0 changed, 0 destroyed.

Outputs:

webserver_ip = 35.227.31.206
```

Figure 4-15. *GCP Terraform code output*

After running `terraform apply`, let's verify the virtual machine instance configuration on the GCP console. Navigate to the VM instance pane (see Figure 4-16) to verify the provisioned instance.

Figure 4-16. *GCP console-level validation of VM instance*

Creating a GCS Bucket with Terraform

Listing 4-8 creates a GCS bucket. We provide all the input variable details in the vars.tf file shown in Listing 4-9. The provider.tf file contains the project details.

Listing 4-8. Provider.tf

```
variable "project" {
  type        = string
  default     = "your project id"
  description = "GCP Project to be used for creating resources"
}
```

Listing 4-9. Vars.tf

```
variable "name" {
  description = "The name of the bucket."
  type        = string
  default     = "terrahashi"
}
variable "location" {
  description = "The location of the bucket."
  type        = string
  default     = "us-east1"
}

variable "storage_class" {
  description = "The Storage Class of the new bucket."
  type        = string
  default     = "STANDARD"
}

variable "labels" {
  description = "A set of key/value label pairs to assign to
                the bucket."
  type        = map(string)
  default     = null
}
```

```
variable "bucket_policy_only" {
  description = "Enables Bucket Policy Only access to a bucket."
  type        = bool
  default     = true
}

variable "versioning" {
  description = "While set to true, versioning is fully enabled
                 for this bucket."
  type        = bool
  default     = true
}

variable "force_destroy" {
  description = "When deleting a bucket, this boolean option
                 will delete all contained objects. If false,
                 Terraform will fail to delete buckets which
                 contain objects."
  type        = bool
  default     = false
}

variable "retention_policy" {
  description            = "Configuration of the bucket's data
                            retention policy for how long objects in
                            the bucket should be retained."
  type                   = object({
    is_locked        = bool
    retention_period = number
  })
  default = null
}
```

```
variable "encryption" {
  description = "A Cloud KMS key that will be used to encrypt
                objects inserted into this bucket"
  type        = object({
    default_kms_key_name = string
  })
  default = null
}
```

The main.tf file keeps the logical configuration of the components used to provision GCS with its retention policy and lifecycle rule, as shown in Listing 4-10.

Listing 4-10. Main.tf

```
provider "google" {
  project     = var.project
  credentials = file("#########################.json")  // your
  credentials.json to be used here
}

#---------------------------------------------
# Creating GCS Bucket
#---------------------------------------------

resource "google_storage_bucket" "bucket" {
  name                        = var.name
  project                     = var.project
  location                    = var.location
  storage_class               = var.storage_class
  uniform_bucket_level_access = var.bucket_policy_only
  labels                      = var.labels
  force_destroy               = var.force_destroy
```

```
 versioning {
   enabled = var.versioning
 }
dynamic "retention_policy" {
  for_each = var.retention_policy == null ? [] : [var.
  retention_policy]
  content {
    is_locked        = var.retention_policy.is_locked
    retention_period = var.retention_policy.retention_period
  }
}

dynamic "encryption" {
  for_each = var.encryption == null ? [] : [var.encryption]
  content {
    default_kms_key_name = var.encryption.default_kms_key_name
  }
}

lifecycle_rule {
    action {
      type         = "SetStorageClass"
      storage_class = "NEARLINE"
    }
    condition {
        age = 7
    }
  }
lifecycle_rule {
    action {
      type         = "SetStorageClass"
      storage_class = "COLDLINE"
    }
```

```
    condition {
      age = 30
    }
  }
}
```

The output.tf file displays the bucket name with information about its specifications and configurations (see Listing 4-11).

Listing 4-11. Output.tf

```
output "bucket" {
  description = "The created storage bucket"
  value       = google_storage_bucket.bucket
}
```

Run `terraform init`, `plan`, and `apply` to create the GCS bucket. The output is shown in Figure 4-17.

```
google_storage_bucket.bucket: Creating...
google_storage_bucket.bucket: Creation complete after 4s [id=terrazion]

Apply complete! Resources: 1 added, 0 changed, 0 destroyed.

Outputs:

bucket = [
  "bucket_policy_only" = true
  "cors" = []
  "default_event_based_hold" = false
  "encryption" = []
  "force_destroy" = false
  "id" = "terrazion"
  "lifecycle_rule" = [
    {
      "action" = [
        {
          "storage_class" = "NEARLINE"
          "type" = "SetStorageClass"
        },
      ]
      "condition" = [
        {
          "age" = 7
          "created_before" = ""
          "matches_storage_class" = []
          "num_newer_versions" = 0
          "with_state" = "ANY"
        },
      ]
    },
    {
      "action" = [
        {
          "storage_class" = "COLDLINE"
          "type" = "SetStorageClass"
        },
      ]
      "condition" = [
        {
          "age" = 30
          "created_before" = ""
          "matches_storage_class" = []
```

Figure 4-17. *GCP Terraform code output*

After running the three use cases for the VPC/subnet, virtual instance, and GCS bucket, you can execute `terraform destroy` in the respective code directories to clean all the resources, as shown in Figure 4-18.

```
google_storage_bucket.bucket: Refreshing state... [id=terrazion]

An execution plan has been generated and is shown below.
Resource actions are indicated with the following symbols:
    destroy

Terraform will perform the following actions:

  # google_storage_bucket.bucket will be destroyed
  - resource "google_storage_bucket" "bucket" {
      - bucket_policy_only          = true
      - default_event_based_hold    = false
      - force_destroy               = false
      - id                          = "terrazion"
      - labels                      = {}
      - location                    = "US-EAST1"
      - name                        = "terrazion"
      - project                     = "crafty-student-290205"
      - requester_pays              = false
      - self_link                   = "https://www.googleapis.com/storage/v1/b/terrazion"
      - storage_class               = "STANDARD"
      - uniform_bucket_level_access = true
      - url                         = "gs://terrazion"

      - lifecycle_rule {
          - action {
              - storage_class = "NEARLINE"
              - type          = "SetStorageClass"
            }

          - condition {
              - age                 = 7
              - matches_storage_class = []
              - num_newer_versions  = 0
              - with_state          = "ANY"
            }
        }
      - lifecycle_rule {
          - action {
              - storage_class = "COLDLINE"
              - type          = "SetStorageClass"
```

Figure 4-18. *GCP terraform destroy*

Automating the Azure Public Cloud Using Terraform

To use services on the Microsoft Azure cloud, you must have an Azure account. This section explains how to create a Microsoft account for Terraform integration. Microsoft Azure offers a free 30-day trial for all new accounts.

Navigate to https://azure.microsoft.com and create a free account to begin using Azure cloud services.

Click the Start Free button to begin the free trial subscription. Enter your email address and password.

Enter your information in all the fields required to create the account, and then click Next (see Figure 4-19).

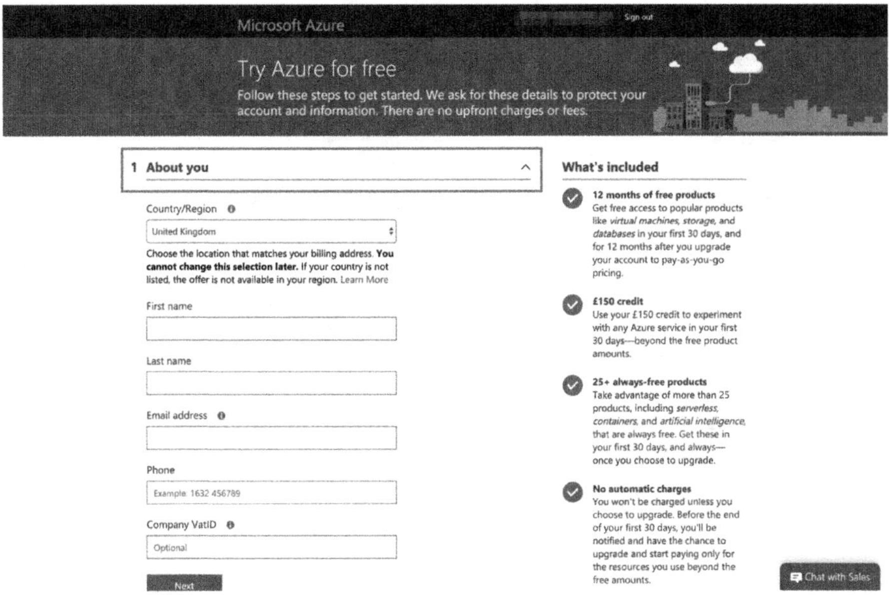

Figure 4-19.   *Provide details for account creation*

Confirm your identification via phone call or text message per the information provided in the previous step. Enter your credit card information for verification, as shown in Figure 4-20.

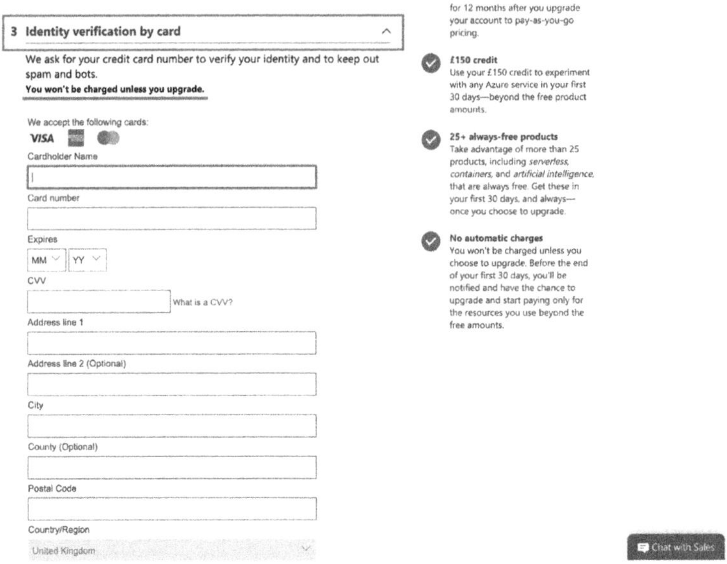

Figure 4-20. *Credit card information for account creation*

Select the checkboxes to accept Microsoft Azure's terms and conditions. Click the Sign Up button to complete the account creation process (see Figure 4-21).

Figure 4-21. *Complete sign-up process*

Navigate to `https://login.microsoftonline.com` to log in to your Azure account using the Azure portal.

The next step is to create an Azure service principal that integrates Terraform with Azure. Navigate to Azure Active Directory → App registrations and click the +New Application Registration button, as shown in Figure 4-22.

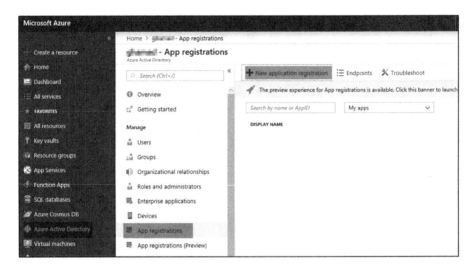

Figure 4-22. *Creating a service principal*

Provide a name and URL (test.com) for the application. Select Web app/API as the type of application (see Figure 4-23). After setting the values, click the Create button.

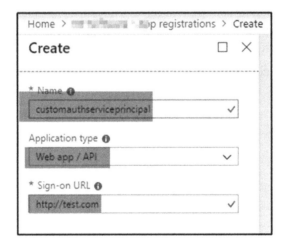

Figure 4-23. *Providing details for service principal*

Once registration is completed, note the application ID and tenant ID (see Figure 4-24). These values are used for integration.

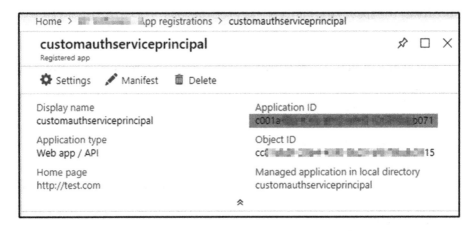

Figure 4-24. *Service principal*

Figure 4-25 shows the Azure services that we automated using Terraform. For this exercise, we create a VNet (virtual network), subnet, NSG, and virtual machine using Terraform. Let's begin the exercise.

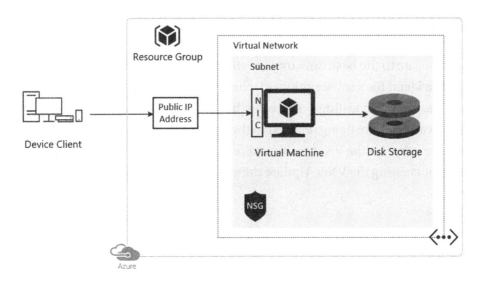

Figure 4-25. *Azure hands-on exercise*

Clone the files from the GitHub repository used in this exercise by using the following command.

git clone https://github.com/dryice-devops/Terraform-Azure-UseCase-Automation/tree/master

You see the directory structure under the cloned directory, as shown in Figure 4-26.

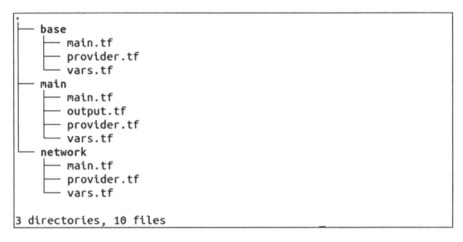

```
.
├── base
│   ├── main.tf
│   ├── provider.tf
│   └── vars.tf
├── main
│   ├── main.tf
│   ├── output.tf
│   ├── provider.tf
│   └── vars.tf
└── network
    ├── main.tf
    ├── provider.tf
    └── vars.tf

3 directories, 10 files
```

Figure 4-26. *Clone Terraform directories*

Navigate to the base directory (as shown in Figure 4-26) and update the provider.tf file's subscription_id, client_id, client_secret, and tenant_id fields, as shown in Listing 4-12 (using the service principal information). These variables are being referred to the provider.tf file. Also, update the variable value for the VNet name and resource group name and location used for creating the VNet. Update the vars.tf file (see Listing 4-13).

Listing 4-12. Update Provider.tf File

```
variable "subscription_id" {
  type        = string
  default     = "Enter Subscription ID"
  description = "Specifies the ID of the Subscription"
}

variable "client_id" {
  type        = string
  default     = "Enter Client ID"
  description = "Specifies the ID of the Azure Client"
}

variable "client_secret" {
  type        = string
  default     = "Enter client_secret"
  description = "Specifies the Client Secret"
}

variable "tenant_id" {
  type        = string
  default     = "Enter Tenant ID"
  description = "Specifies the ID of the Tenant"
}

variable "location" {
  type        = string
  default     = "West US"
  description = "The Location/Region where the Virtual network
                is created"
}
```

Listing 4-13. Vars.tf File

```
variable "vnet_name" {
  type        = string
  default     = "Test"
  description = "The name of the Vnet to be used in VM Scale Set"
}
```

Let's review the main.tf file, which contains details of the VNet provisioned using Terraform (see Listing 4-14). Azure Virtual Network, or VNet, is the fundamental building block for your resources, which are running in a private network. VNet enables many types of Azure resources (e.g., virtual machines) to securely communicate with each other.

Listing 4-14. VNet Terraform Main.tf File

```
############### Creating Resource group ###################

resource "azurerm_resource_group" "demo" {
  name     = var.rg_name
  location = var.location
}

############### Creating virtual Network ###################

resource "azurerm_virtual_network" "demo" {
  name                = var.vnet_name
  address_space       = ["10.0.0.0/16"]
  location            = var.location
  resource_group_name = var.rg_name
  depends_on          = [azurerm_resource_group.demo]
```

Run terraform init, plan, and apply to create Azure VNet. The output is shown in Figure 4-27.

```
Initializing the backend...

Initializing provider plugins...
- Checking for available provider plugins...
- Downloading plugin for provider "azurerm" (hashicorp/azurerm) 2.32.0...

Terraform has been successfully initialized!

You may now begin working with Terraform. Try running "terraform plan" to see
any changes that are required for your infrastructure. All Terraform commands
should now work.

If you ever set or change modules or backend configuration for Terraform,
rerun this command to reinitialize your working directory. If you forget, other
commands will detect it and remind you to do so if necessary.
```

```
Plan: 2 to add, 0 to change, 0 to destroy.

Do you want to perform these actions?
  Terraform will perform the actions described above.
  Only 'yes' will be accepted to approve.

  Enter a value: yes

azurerm_resource_group.demo: Creating...
azurerm_resource_group.demo: Creation complete after 4s [id=/subscriptions/3
azurerm_virtual_network.demo: Creating...
azurerm_virtual_network.demo: Still creating... [10s elapsed]
azurerm_virtual_network.demo: Creation complete after 14s [id=/subscriptions
work/virtualNetworks/demo-network]

Apply complete! Resources: 2 added, 0 changed, 0 destroyed.
```

Figure 4-27. *VNet Terraform execution*

After successful provisioning, you can validate the VNet configuration
using the Azure portal (see Figure 4-28).

117

Figure 4-28. *VNet validation from Azure portal*

Now that our resource group and VNet have been created, let's begin creating a subnet and NSG using Terraform.

Navigate to the network directory (as shown in Figure 4-26) and update the var.tf file's subscription_id, client_id, client_secret, and tenant_id fields (see Listing 4-15), using the service principal information). These variables are referred to in the provider.tf file. Also, update the variable value for the subnet name, VNet name, resource group name (use the name of the resource group used for the VNet use case), and the name and location used to create the subnet and NSG. The NSG rule and subnet prefix sizes are already defined in the main.tf file (see Listing 4-16). A network security group contains security rules that allow or deny inbound and outbound traffic from several types of Azure resources.

Listing 4-15. Vars and Provider File

```
variable "subscription_id" {
  type        = string
  default     = "Enter Subscription ID"
  description = "Specifies the ID of the Subscription"
}
```

```
variable "client_id" {
  type        = string
  default     = "Enter Client ID"
  description = "Specifies the ID of the Azure Client"
}

variable "client_secret" {
  type        = string
  default     = "Enter client_secret"
  description = "Specifies the Client Secret"
}

variable "tenant_id" {
  type        = string
  default     = "Enter Tenant ID"
  description = "Specifies the ID of the Tenant"
}

variable "location" {
  type        = string
  default     = "West US"
  description = "The Location/Region where the Virtual network
                 is created"
}

variable "rg_name" {
  type        = string
  default     = "Test"
  description = "The name of the Resource Group where the
                 Resource will be Created"
}
```

```
variable "subnet_name" {
  type        = string
  default     = "Test"
  description = "The name of the Subnet to be used in VM
                Scale Set"
}

variable "vnet_name" {
  type        = string
  default     = "Test"
  description = "The name of the Subnet to be used in VM
                Scale Set"
}

variable "nsg_name" {
  type        = string
  default     = "Test"
  description = "The name of the Network Security Group to be
                used to InBound and OutBound Traffic"
}
```

Listing 4-16. Subnet prefix and NSG definitions in Main.tf File

```
############### Creating Subnet #########################

resource "azurerm_subnet" "demo" {
  name                 = var.subnet_name
  address_prefix       = ["10.0.2.0/24"]
  resource_group_name  = var.rg_name
  virtual_network_name = var.vnet_name
}
```

```
################# Creating NSG and Rule ####################
resource "azurerm_network_security_group" "demo" {
  name                = var.nsg_name
  resource_group_name = var.rg_name
  location            = var.location
    security_rule {
    name                       = "HTTP"
    priority                   = 1020
    direction                  = "Inbound"
    access                     = "allow"
    protocol                   = "tcp"
    source_port_range          = "*"
    destination_port_range     = "80"
    source_address_prefix      = "*"
    destination_address_prefix = "*"
    }
tags = {
    ENVIRONMENT = "Terraform Demo"
    }
```

Run terraform init, plan, and apply to create an Azure subnet and NSG. The output is shown in Figure 4-29.

```
# azurerm_subnet.demo will be created
+ resource "azurerm_subnet" "demo" {
    + address_prefix                                 = "10.0.2.0/24"
    + address_prefixes                               = (known after apply)
    + enforce_private_link_endpoint_network_policies = false
    + enforce_private_link_service_network_policies  = false
    + id                                             = (known after apply)
    + name                                           = "demo"
    + resource_group_name                            = "demo"
    + virtual_network_name                           = "demo"
  }

Plan: 2 to add, 0 to change, 0 to destroy.


Warning: "address_prefix": [DEPRECATED] Use the `address_prefixes` property instead.

  on main.tf line 2, in resource "azurerm_subnet" "demo":
   2: resource "azurerm_subnet" "demo" {


Do you want to perform these actions?
  Terraform will perform the actions described above.
  Only 'yes' will be accepted to approve.

  Enter a value: yes

azurerm_subnet.demo: Creating...
azurerm_network_security_group.demo: Creating...
azurerm_subnet.demo: Creation complete after 6s [id=/subscriptions/3f853c29-f9c0-42b
alNetworks/demo/subnets/demo]
azurerm_network_security_group.demo: Still creating... [10s elapsed]
azurerm_network_security_group.demo: Creation complete after 13s [id=/subscriptions/
oft.Network/networkSecurityGroups/demo]

Apply complete! Resources: 2 added, 0 changed, 0 destroyed.
```

Figure 4-29. *Subnet and NSG Terraform execution*

Now that our resource group and VNet have been created, let's extend the code to create a public IP, network interface, and a virtual machine. We used the VNet and subnet from other Terraform function data.

Now that the VNet, subnet, and NSG have been created, let's create a virtual machine using Terraform. All the configurations are defined in the main.tf file shown in Listing 4-17. All the variables are defined in Listing 4-18.

Listing 4-17. Main.tf

```
########## Fetch Info of existing Resources ###################

data "azurerm_subnet" subnet {
  name                 = var.subnet_name
  resource_group_name  = var.rg_name
  virtual_network_name = var.vnet_name
}

data "azurerm_network_security_group" "nsg" {
  name                = var.nsg_name
  resource_group_name = var.rg_name
}

############# Create Public Ip ###############################

resource "azurerm_public_ip" "demo" {
  name                = var.pip_name
  location            = var.location
  resource_group_name = var.rg_name
  allocation_method   = "Static"

  tags = {
      ENVIRONMENT = "Terraform Demo"
  }
}

############# Create Network Interface ########################

resource "azurerm_network_interface" "demo" {
  name = var.network_int_name
  location = var.location
  resource_group_name = var.rg_name
```

```
 ip_configuration {
     name = "demo"
     subnet_id = data.azurerm_subnet.subnet.id
     private_ip_address_allocation = "Dynamic"
     public_ip_address_id = azurerm_public_ip.demo.id
 }
 tags = {
     ENVIRONMENT = "Terraform Demo"
 }
}

#### Connect the Security Groups to the network interface ####

resource "azurerm_network_interface_security_group_association"
"demo" {
  network_interface_id = azurerm_network_interface.demo.id
  network_security_group_id = data.azurerm_network_security_
  group.nsg.id
}

############# Create virtual Machine ########################

resource "azurerm_virtual_machine" "demo" {
  name = "demo-vm"
  location = var.location
  resource_group_name = var.rg_name
  network_interface_id = [azurerm_network_interface.demo.id]
  vm_size = var.node_size

  storage_image_reference {
    publisher = "Canonical"
    offer = "UbuntuServer"
    sku = "16.04-LTS"
    version = "latest"
  }
```

```
storage_os_disk {
  name = "demoosdisk"
  caching = "ReadWrite"
  create_option = "FromImage"
  managed_disk_type = "Standard_LRS"
}

os_profile {
  computer_name = "demo-vm"
  admin_username = var.username
  admin_password = var.password
}

os_profile_linux_config {
  disable_password_authentication = false
}

tags = {
  ENVIRONMENT = "Terraform Demo"
}
}
```

Listing 4-18. Vars.tf

```
variable "vnet_name" {
  type        = string
  default     = "Test"
  description = "The name of the Vnet to be used in VM Scale Set"
}
```

```
variable "subnet_name" {
  type        = string
  default     = "Test"
  description = "The name of the Subnet to be used in VM
                Scale Set"
}

variable "nsg_name" {
  type        = string
  default     = "Test"
  description = "The name of the Network Security Group to be
                used to InBound and OutBound Traffic"
}

variable "pip_name" {
  type        = string
  default     = "Test"
  description = "The name of the Public Ip for accessing VM"
}

variable "network_int_name" {
  type        = string
  default     = "Test"
  description = "The name of the Network interface"
}

variable "node_size" {
  type        = string
  default     = "Standard_DS1_v2"
  description = "The size of the Azure VM Node"
}
```

```
variable "username" {
  type        = string
  default     = "SU-user"
  description = "The name of the user for VM Login"
}

variable "password" {
  type        = string
  default     = "#YLPRgg89"
  description = "The password of the user for VM Login"
}
```

Run terraform init, plan, and apply to create the Azure VM, NIC, and Public IP. The output is shown in Figure 4-30.

```
Plan: 4 to add, 0 to change, 0 to destroy.

Do you want to perform these actions?
  Terraform will perform the actions described above.
  Only 'yes' will be accepted to approve.

  Enter a value: yes

azurerm_public_ip.demo: Creating...
azurerm_public_ip.demo: Still creating... [10s elapsed]
azurerm_public_ip.demo: Creation complete after 11s [id=/subscriptions/3
ublicIPAddresses/demo]
azurerm_network_interface.demo: Creating...
azurerm_network_interface.demo: Still creating... [10s elapsed]
azurerm_network_interface.demo: Creation complete after 11s [id=/subscri
etwork/networkInterfaces/demo]
azurerm_network_interface_security_group_association.demo: Creating...
azurerm_virtual_machine.demo: Creating...
azurerm_network_interface_security_group_association.demo: Creation compl
demo/providers/Microsoft.Network/networkInterfaces/demo|/subscriptions/3
etworkSecurityGroups/demo]
azurerm_virtual_machine.demo: Still creating... [10s elapsed]
azurerm_virtual_machine.demo: Still creating... [20s elapsed]
azurerm_virtual_machine.demo: Still creating... [30s elapsed]
azurerm_virtual_machine.demo: Still creating... [40s elapsed]
azurerm_virtual_machine.demo: Still creating... [50s elapsed]
azurerm_virtual_machine.demo: Still creating... [1m0s elapsed]
azurerm_virtual_machine.demo: Creation complete after 1m3s [id=/subscript
mpute/virtualMachines/demo-vm]

Apply complete! Resources: 4 added, 0 changed, 0 destroyed.

Outputs:

public_ip_address_demo = 13.64.128.215
```

Figure 4-30. *Virtual machine Terraform execution*

After successful provisioning, you can also validate the virtual machine configuration using the Azure portal (see Figure 4-31).

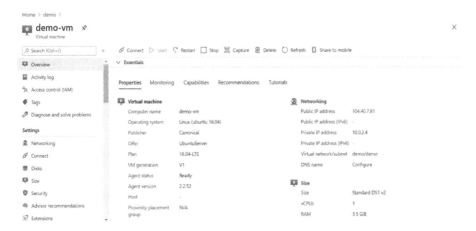

Figure 4-31. *Virtual machine validation in Azure portal*

After completing the exercise, be sure to clean up all resources by executing `terraform destroy` for the virtual machine, subnet, NSG, and VNet.

Summary

This chapter provided hands-on exercises for automating Azure and GCP services using open source Terraform.

The next chapter covers a HashiCorp Vault solution and how it manages secrets in IaC automation scenarios using Terraform.

CHAPTER 5

Getting Started with Vault

This chapter covers the core concepts of Vault.

- Introduction to HashiCorp Vault

- Understanding Vault's logical architecture

- Understanding Vault's security model

- Installing Vault and integration with AWS

Note In this chapter, all references to Vault are for the open source version. Thus, features like disaster recovery, enterprise governance, compliance, and replication across DCs are not explained because they are associated with the Enterprise version of Vault.

Introduction to HashiCorp Vault

HashiCorp Vault is used for storing and securely accessing secrets. You can access the secrets using API keys and passwords. Secrets are defined as any form of sensitive credentials that need to be controlled and can be used to unlock sensitive information. Secrets in Vault could be of any type,

© Navin Sabharwal, Sarvesh Pandey and Piyush Pandey 2021

N. Sabharwal et al., *Infrastructure-as-Code Automation Using Terraform, Packer, Vault, Nomad and Consul*, https://doi.org/10.1007/978-1-4842-7129-2_5

including sensitive environment variables, database credentials, API keys, RSA tokens, and more.

Protecting secrets and access in automation is of primary importance. Vault makes it easy to manage secrets and access by leveraging APIs and a user-friendly interface. You can monitor detailed logs and fetch the audit trail describing who accessed which secrets and when.

User authentication to Vault can either be via password or using dynamic values to generate temporary tokens that allows a particular user to access a secret. Policies can also be defined using HashiCorp Configuration Language (HCL) to determine which user gets what level of access.

The following are Vault's key features.

- **Data encryption:** Vault can easily encrypt and decrypt credentials. It provides a security configuration feature to define encryption parameters, and developers can store encrypted data in it without having to design their own encryption methods.

- **Revocation:** Vault provides a default feature that revokes credentials after a fixed duration (768 hours). This value is configurable and can be set per user requirements. Revocation assists in key and secret rotation and locking down systems in the event of an intrusion.

Note   The leasing method of dynamic credentials ensures that Vault knows each client's secrets. This makes it possible to revoke specific leases in any attack/hacking attempt.

- **On-demand secrets:** Vault can generate on-demand secrets for few methods (e.g., AWS or SQL database). It can handle dynamic secrets, which are generated on demand basis. A secret ID is unique for a particular user. Dynamic secrets are more secure than static secrets, which are predefined and shared. Vault can revoke access when the lease expires for on-demand secrets.

- **Renewal:** Vault has a secret renewal feature. It can revoke credentials, and end users can renew secrets through the renew API. By attaching a lease period to secrets, Vault has information on maximum time to live, and after that duration, secrets are automatically rotated.

- **Secret management:** Secret management is one of Vault's primary features. It can store any type of credentials, including sensitive environment variables, API keys, and databases. Vault allows you to take full control of any sensitive secrets used for automating hybrid cloud services.

Understanding Vault's Logical Architecture

Now let's look at the logical architecture of the HashiCorp Vault solution, as shown in Figure 5-1.

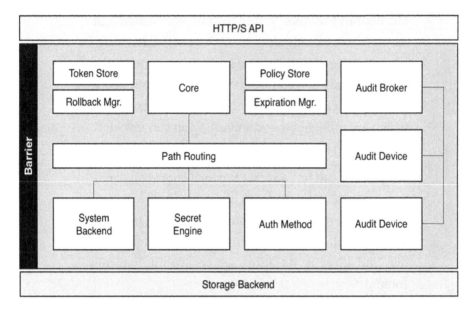

Figure 5-1. *Vault logical architecture*

The following are Vault's key components.

- The **storage backend** stores encrypted data/secrets.

- A **barrier** is used for all data flows between Vault and backend storage.

- A **client token** verifies the identity of the end user.

- A **secret** controls access (e.g., passwords).

- An **auth method** authenticates the application and users connecting to Vault.

Figure 5-2 shows a high-level flow between an admin or application and Vault for accessing secrets. It is used for managing secrets; you can secure your credentials with Vault.

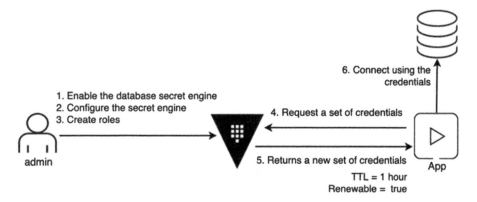

Figure 5-2. *Application and Vault architecture*

While applications can request secrets from Vault based on the policy configured for access and secret management, the admin can define the backend policies for secret lifecycle governance.

Understanding Vault's Security Model

Vault security architecture is designed to meet the key infosec controls i.e. confidentiality, integrity, availability, accountability, and authorized access using authentication. Vault helps prevent eavesdropping or tampering attempts by leveraging data at rest and transit encryption techniques. A similar approach is used to protect data in backend storage leveraged for secrets.

Now let's look at the threat vector or paths of intrusion and see how Vault helps protect secrets from such threats. Essentially, there are two kinds of threats: external and internal.

Vault securely manages sensitive data. Its security model is leveraged to ensure authentication, availability, and integrity to secure sensitive data. End user or application access to data is governed by a robust authentication and authorization model and policies to provide granular control for security and access management.

As shown in Figure 5-3, there are three different systems that are of concern when it comes to accessing Vault.

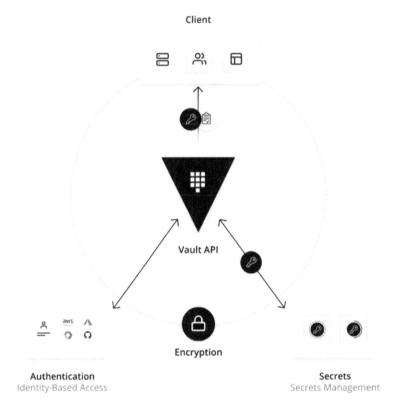

Figure 5-3. *Managing secrets and protecting sensitive data*

The client, an application or automation code, accesses Vault using an API or CLI interface to access a secret. Clients use secure TLS-based connections to verify the server's identity and establish a secure communication channel with Vault. The server requires that the client provide a client token for each Vault access request in order to identify the client. A client that does not provide its own token is not allowed any login or secret access. Vault communicates with the backend over TLS to provide an additional layer of security.

End users sometimes worry that attackers may hack Vault's system data despite robust authentication and authorization features. Within the traditional Vault systems, a major security concern is that attackers may successfully access secret material that they are not authorized to access. This kind of threat is an internal threat.

When a client first authenticates, an auth method verifies the client's identity and, in return, gets a list of associated ACL policies. This association is primarily configured by the administrators or operators.

Figure 5-4 shows that if an application wants to communicate with sensitive data, Vault creates a randomly generated token for authentication.

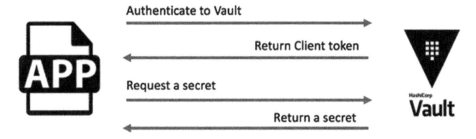

Figure 5-4. *App integrates with Vault data*

The application sends a token upon receiving each request for communication. Vault checks the validity of the token for communication and generates an ACL based on the associated policies. Based on the ACL policy rule, the application performs many actions.

Installing Vault CLI and Integration with AWS

Let's install HashiCorp Vault CLI and see how it works in a hands-on exercise where we will use AWS public cloud secrets for managing secrets.

Before installing Vault, you need an AWS S3 bucket to be created and an AWS KMS service to be set up first. This is used later in another hands-on exercise. Let's use the same AWS account created in Chapter 2 for the S3 bucket.

Sign in to the AWS console and navigate to S3 services under Storage and Content Delivery. Click the Create Bucket button and provide the name and region information to create the bucket, as shown in Figure 5-5.

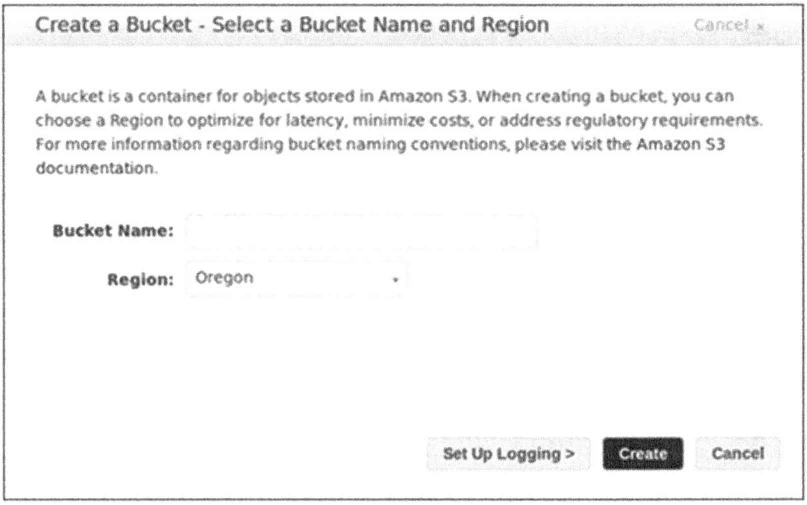

Figure 5-5. *Create S3 bucket*

Note   While performing the hands on execercise we assume user has KMS keys with IAM user permission to integrate with the Vault setup.

To install Vault, you need a virtual machine with the Linux operating system. We are using CentOS for our hands-on exercise however HashiCorp Vault also supports other Linux flavors like Ubuntu, RHEL and Debian. Execute the following command to install the yum-utils package used to manage the package repository on a Linux system (see Figure 5-6).

```
sudo yum install -y yum-utils
```

```
[centos@demo ~]$ sudo yum install -y yum-utils
Loaded plugins: fastestmirror
Determining fastest mirrors
epel/x86_64/metalink
 * base: d36uatko69830t.cloudfront.net
 * epel: download-cc-rdu01.fedoraproject.org
 * extras: d36uatko69830t.cloudfront.net
 * updates: d36uatko69830t.cloudfront.net
base
epel
extras
updates
(1/7): base/7/x86_64/group_gz
```

Figure 5-6. *Install yum-utils*

Execute the following command to add the HashiCorp repository to install Vault using the yum-config manager (see Figure 5-7).

```
sudo yum-config-manager –add-repo https://rpm.releases.
hashicorp.com/RHEL/hashicorp.repo
```

```
[centos@demo ~]$ sudo yum-config-manager --add-repo https://rpm.releases.hashicorp.com/RHEL/hashicorp.repo
Loaded plugins: fastestmirror
adding repo from: https://rpm.releases.hashicorp.com/RHEL/hashicorp.repo
grabbing file https://rpm.releases.hashicorp.com/RHEL/hashicorp.repo to /etc/yum.repos.d/hashicorp.repo
repo saved to /etc/yum.repos.d/hashicorp.repo
```

Figure 5-7. *Add HashiCorp repository*

Execute the following command to install Vault on the Linux server, as shown in Figure 5-8.

```
sudo yum -y install vault
```

```
[centos@demo ~]$ sudo yum -y install vault
Loaded plugins: fastestmirror
Loading mirror speeds from cached hostfile
 * base: d36uatko69830t.cloudfront.net
 * epel: download-cc-rdu01.fedoraproject.org
 * extras: d36uatko69830t.cloudfront.net
 * updates: d36uatko69830t.cloudfront.net
hashicorp
hashicorp/7/x86_64/primary
hashicorp
Resolving Dependencies
--> Running transaction check
---> Package vault.x86_64 0:1.5.4-1 will be installed
```

Figure 5-8. *Installation of Vault*

Execute the following commands to verify Vault installation (see Figures 5-9, 5-10, and 5-11).

```
vault --help
```

```
[centos@demo ~]$ vault --help
Usage: vault <command> [args]

Common commands:
    read          Read data and retrieves secrets
    write         Write data, configuration, and secrets
    delete        Delete secrets and configuration
    list          List data or secrets
    login         Authenticate locally
    agent         Start a Vault agent
    server        Start a Vault server
    status        Print seal and HA status
    unwrap        Unwrap a wrapped secret

Other commands:
    audit         Interact with audit devices
    auth          Interact with auth methods
    debug         Runs the debug command
    kv            Interact with Vault's Key-Value storage
    lease         Interact with leases
    monitor       Stream log messages from a Vault server
    namespace     Interact with namespaces
    operator      Perform operator-specific tasks
    path-help     Retrieve API help for paths
    plugin        Interact with Vault plugins and catalog
    policy        Interact with policies
    print         Prints runtime configurations
    secrets       Interact with secrets engines
    ssh           Initiate an SSH session
    token         Interact with tokens
```

Figure 5-9. *Verify Vault installation*

```
vault --version
```

```
[centos@demo ~]$ vault --version
Vault v1.5.4 (1a730771ec70149293efe91e1d283b10d255c6d1)
```

Figure 5-10. *Verify Vault version*

```
sudo service vault status
```

```
[centos@demo ~]$ sudo service vault status
Redirecting to /bin/systemctl status vault.service
● vault.service - "HashiCorp Vault - A tool for managing secrets"
   Loaded: loaded (/usr/lib/systemd/system/vault.service; disabled; vendor preset: disabled)
   Active: inactive (dead)
     Docs: https://www.vaultproject.io/docs/
```

Figure 5-11. *Verify service status*

Now let's access the Vault UI. Before that you need to update the Vault config file and disable HTTPS access for the lab exercise. This feature is typically enabled in a production or customer environment however in this lab exercise we are disabling the feature to avoid any certificate errors in HTTPS-based access.

Navigate to /etc/vault.d path and edit the vault.hcl file by uncommenting the HTTP listener block and commenting out HTTPS listener block (see Figure 5-12).

```
# HTTP listener
Listener "tcp" {
  address = "0.0.0.0:8200"
  tls_disable = 1
}

#HTTPS listerner
#listener "tcp" {
#   address = "0.0.0.0:8200"
#   tls_cert_file = "/opt/vault/tls/tls.crt"
#   tls_key_file = "/opt/vault/tls/tls.key"
#}
```

Figure 5-12. *Disable HTTPS listener*

Save the /etc/vault.d/vault.hcl file after making the changes, and restart Vault. After restarting the Vault service, access the UI at http:// <IP address of your Vault server>:8200/ui/vault/init (see Figure 5-13).

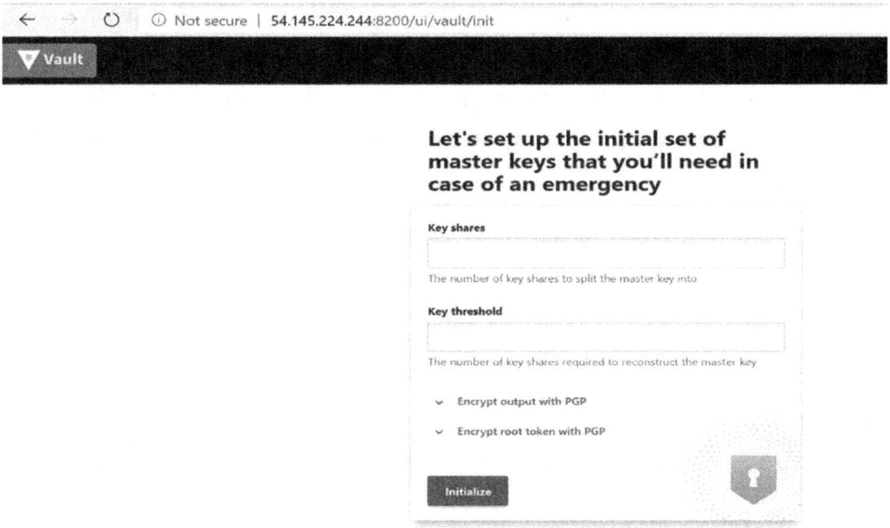

Figure 5-13. *Check Vault UI*

Execute the following commands to set the VAULT_ADDR variable and check the Vault server status (see Figure 5-14).

```
export VAULT_ADDR='http://127.0.0.1:8200'
vault status
```

```
[centos@demo ~]$ export VAULT_ADDR='http://127.0.0.1:8200'
[centos@demo ~]$ vault  status
Key                Value
---                -----
Seal Type          shamir
Initialized        false
Sealed             true
Total Shares       0
Threshold          0
Unseal Progress    0/0
Unseal Nonce       n/a
Version            n/a
HA Enabled         false
```

Figure 5-14. *Check Vault status*

Now let's integrate the S3 bucket created earlier as a backend for Vault. Navigate to /etc/vault.d path and edit the vault.hcl file to provide information on the AWS S3 bucket name, the bucket region, KMS ID, and the access-secret keys (see Figures 5-15(a), 5-15(b), and 5-16). Save the file and restart Vault.

```
#Example of vault.hcl file

ui = true

#mlock = true
#disable_mlock = true

Storage "file" {
  Path = "/opt/vault/data"
}
```

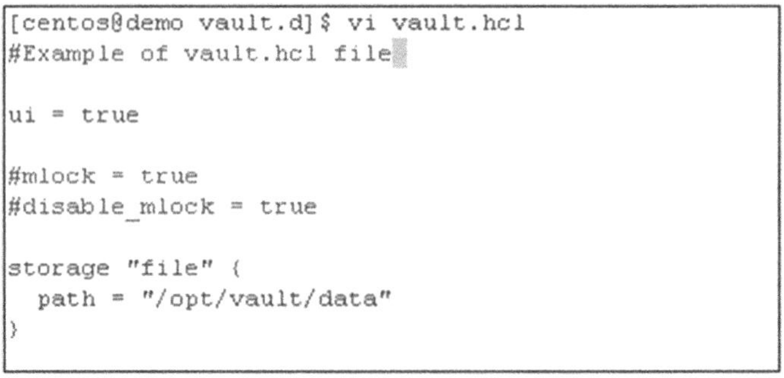

Figure 5-15(a). *Navigate to /etc/vault.d and edit vault.hcl file*

```
storage "s3" {
  access_key = "Enter Access Key"
  secret_key = "Enter Secret Keys"
  bucket     = "Add bucket name"
  region     = "Enter Aws Region"
}
```

```
storage "s3" {
  access_key = "Enter Access Key"
  secret_key = "Enter Secret Keys"
  bucket     = "Add bucket name"
  region     = "Enter Aws Region"
}
```

Figure 5-15(b). *Update config file for S3*

```
storage "awskms" {
  access_key = "Enter Access Key"
  secret_key = "Enter Secret Keys"
  region     = "Enter Aws Region"
  kms_key_id = "Enter KMS ID"
}
```

```
# Example AWS KMS auto unseal
seal "awskms" {
  access_key = "Enter Access Key"
  secret_key = "Enter Secret Keys"
  region = "Enter Aws Region"
  kms_key_id = "Enter KMS ID"
}
```

Figure 5-16. *Update config file with KMS values*

Execute the following command to check Vault status. It now displays an AWS KMS recovery seal, as shown in Figure 5-17.

```
vault status
```

145

```
[centos@demo ~]$ vault status
Key                         Value
---                         -----
Recovery Seal Type          awskms
Initialized                 false
Sealed                      true
Total Recovery Shares       0
Threshold                   0
Unseal Progress             0/0
Unseal Nonce                n/a
Version                     n/a
HA Enabled                  false
```

Figure 5-17. *Check Vault status*

Execute the following command to initialize the Vault server, as shown in Figure 5-18. Copy the root token returned as an output of the command. We use this value later in the exercise.

vault operator init –recovery-shares=1 –recovery-threshold=1

```
[centos@demo ~]$ vault operator init –recovery-shares=1 –recovery-threshold=1
Recovery Key 1: thckdbEaouMj3f0zZZlohfwMFwJePf5b6s9mKgKpRcw=

Initial Root Token: s.scjzhjIrPHHgTwKO4t7MLBGZ

Success! Vault is initialized

Recovery key initialized with 1 key shares and a key threshold of 1. Please
securely distribute the key shares printed above.
```

Figure 5-18. *Initialize Vault*

Now execute the following command to verify that the initialization status is true and the sealed status is false (see Figure 5-19).

```
vault status
```

```
[centos@demo ~]$ vault status
Key                          Value
---                          -----
Recovery Seal Type           shamir
Initialized                  true
Sealed                       false
Total Recovery Shares        1
Threshold                    1
Version                      1.5.5
Cluster Name                 vault-cluster-77fe5aec
Cluster ID                   32a06084-8a78-57f1-d356-61aa905d324d
HA Enabled                   false
```

Figure 5-19. *Check Vault status*

After the initialization is completed, you can navigate to the AWS console and verify that Vault objects are now stored in the S3 bucket, as shown in Figure 5-20.

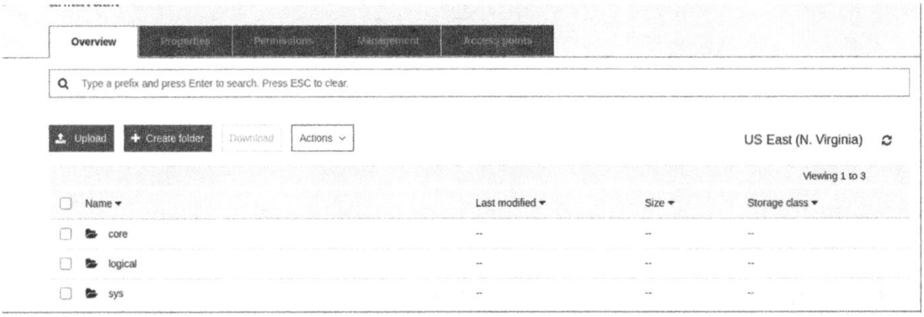

Figure 5-20. *S3 bucket with initialized Vault objects*

Log in to Vault using the root token generated in the previous step by executing the following command, as shown in Figure 5-21.

```
vault login <Your root token>
```

```
[centos@demo ~]$ vault login s.scjzhjIrPHHgTwKO4t7MLBGZ
Success! You are now authenticated. The token information displayed below
is already stored in the token helper. You do NOT need to run "vault login"
again. Future Vault requests will automatically use this token.

Key                     Value
---                     -----
token                   s.scjzhjIrPHHgTwKO4t7MLBGZ
token_accessor          AJOpXuJEMD1QcJz34FHvhUyk
token_duration          â
token_renewable         false
token_policies          ["root"]
identity_policies       []
policies                ["root"]
```

Figure 5-21. *Vault login*

Execute the following command to enable the secret engine, as shown in Figure 5-22.

```
vault secrets enable kv
```

```
[centos@demo ~]$ vault secrets enable kv
Success! Enabled the kv secrets engine at: kv/
```

Figure 5-22. *Enable the secret engine*

Now let's add some basic credentials into the Vault server for testing by executing the following command, as shown in Figure 5-23.

```
vault kv put kv/foo test=mycred
```

```
[centos@demo ~]$ vault kv put kv/foo test=mycred
Success! Data written to: kv/foo
[centos@demo ~]$ vault kv get kv/foo
==== Data ====
Key      Value
---      -----
test     mycred
[centos@demo ~]$
```

Figure 5-23. *Entering credentials to Vault*

You can also validate the credentials added to Vault by logging in to the UI using the token root credentials. Navigate to the Secrets tabs to view details of the foo secret under the key, as shown in Figure 5-24.

Figure 5-24. *Check secrets in Vault UI*

Similarly, you can store multiple types of secrets in Vault, including sensitive environment variables, API keys, RSA tokens, and more.

Now let's add some API keys, as shown in Figure 5-25.

```
vault kv put kv/token token=xxxxxxxx
```

```
[centos@demo vault.d]$ vault kv put kv/token token=xxxxxxx
Success! Data written to: kv/token
```

Figure 5-25. *Adding a token to Vault*

You can validate the token added in the Vault UI, as shown in Figure 5-26.

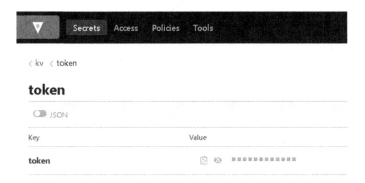

Figure 5-26. *Check token on Vault UI*

You can delete the credentials by executing the following command, as shown in Figure 5-27.

```
vault kv delete kv/foo
```

```
[centos@demo ~]$ vault kv delete kv/foo
Success! Data deleted (if it existed) at: kv/foo
[centos@demo ~]$ vault kv get kv/foo
No value found at kv/foo
[centos@demo ~]$
```

Figure 5-27. *Delete test cred*

Summary

This chapter covered the main concepts of HashiCorp Vault. We learned how to install Vault CLI and performed a hands-on exercise on managing secrets in an AWS public cloud.

The next chapter covers the HashiCorp Packer solution and how it automates image management in a hybrid cloud environment.

CHAPTER 6

Getting Started with HashiCorp Packer

This chapter covers the following HashiCorp Packer topics.

- Introduction to open source HashiCorp Packer

- Installing Packer

- Hands-on exercise in automating AWS AMI creation

Introduction to HashiCorp Packer

Packer is an open source HashiCorp solution for creating machine images for multiple platforms using the IaC methodology. It is a lightweight tool written in the GO language. It has rich integrations for creating machine images with support for multiple platforms in parallel by leveraging a single-source code version-controlled declarative configuration.

Packer capabilities cover two key areas. The first one is building base images for application infrastructure. Packer creates an image that contains all the dependencies, patches, and configurations required to run one or multiple applications. The second one is creating golden images (where everything is baked inside the image). With Packer now Golden image configuration can be automated for initial release as well as future releases can be protected against any configuration drift.

© Navin Sabharwal, Sarvesh Pandey and Piyush Pandey 2021
N. Sabharwal et al., *Infrastructure-as-Code Automation Using Terraform, Packer, Vault, Nomad and Consul*, https://doi.org/10.1007/978-1-4842-7129-2_6

Packer uses a template file that configures the various components used to create one or more machine images. Packer templates consist of the following components.

Builders

The builders block is the engine of the template file. It is responsible for turning templates into a machine and then back into an image for various platforms. Listing 6-1 shows the build section within the Packer template.

Listing 6-1. Builders Block in Packer Template

```
{
    "builders": [
        // ... one or more builder definitions here
    ]
}
```

A simple AWS builders block is shown in the following example. You can define details regarding the AWS AMI in fields like the AMI type, region, and source AMI, from which the image has to be baselined.

```
"builders": [{
    "type": "amazon-ebs",
    "access_key": "{{user `aws_access_key`}}",
    "secret_key": "{{user `aws_secret_key`}}",
    "region": "us-west-1",
    "source_ami": "ami-sd3543ds",
    "instance_type": "t2.medium",
    "ssh_username": "ec2-user",
    "ami_name": "packer-demo {{timestamp}}"
}]
```

Communicators

Communicators are considered the transport layer in Packer. They execute scripts and upload files to machines created from images and are configured within the builder section. Packer supports the following three types of communicators.

- **none** No communicator is used. If this is set, most provisioners cannot be used.

- **ssh** An SSH connection is established to the machine. It is usually the default.

- **winrm** A WinRM connection is established.

Now let's review the following code snippet, which shows an SSH communicator configuration.

```
"ssh_username": "{{ user `aws_ssh_username` }}",
"ssh_password": "{{ user `aws_ssh_password` }}",
"ssh_pty" : "true"
```

If an SSH agent is configured on the host running Packer, and SSH agent authentication is enabled in the communicator config, Packer automatically forwards the SSH agent to the remote host.

Provisioners

Provisioners are optional when it comes to automating image creation using Packer. If no provisioners are defined within a template, then no software (other than the defaults) is installed within the resulting machine images.

Now let's review the code snippet shown in Listing 6-2, which shows a provisioners configuration and a sample configuration using a shell type provisioner for executing demo-script.sh.

Listing 6-2. Provisioners Configuration

```
{
    "provisioners": [
        // ... one or more provisioner definitions here
    ]
}
"provisioners": [{
    "type":  "shell",
    "script":  "demo-script.sh"
}]
```

Post-Processors

Post-processors executes after the builder and provisioner components to execute any post-processing task upon the resulting image. Examples include compressing files, uploading artifacts, and so forth.

Listing 6-3. Post-Processors

```
{
    "post-processors": [
        // ... one or more post-processor definitions here
    ]
}
```

There are three ways to define a post-processor in a template (as shown in Listing 6-3): simple definitions, detailed definitions, and sequence definitions. The simple and detailed definitions are shortcuts for a sequence definition.

A *simple definition* is a string name of the post-processor when no additional configuration is needed. The following is an example.

```
{
    "post-processors": ["compress"]
}
```

A *detailed definition* (JSON object) contains a type field to denote the post-processor. It is used when additional configuration is needed. The following is an example.

```
{
    "post-processors": [
    {
        "type": "compress",
        "format": "tar.gz"
    }]
}
```

A *sequence definition* is a JSON array. The post-processors defined in the array are run in order, with the artifact of each feeding into the next. The following is an example.

```
{
    "post-processors": [
        ["compress", {"type": "upload", "endpoint":
        http://example.com }]
    ]
}
```

Variables

The variables supported by Packer are of 2 types: user-defined and environment variables. The variables block holds all the default variables within a template. The following is an example where we are using an instance_type variable for the EC2 server size and the region variable to provide the AWS region for the image.

```
"variables":     {
    "instance_type": "t2.medium",
    "region": "us-west-1"
    }
```

Using Declared Variables in Templates

The declared variables can be accessed using "{{user `variable-name`}}" syntax.

The following is an example where instead of providing hard-coded values, you can take input from the user when executing the code.

```
"instance_type": "{{user `instance_type`}}",
"region": "{{user `region`}}"
```

Using Environment Variables in Templates

Packer lets us use the system's environment variables. You need to declare the environment variables in the variable section to use them in other parts of the template. You can declare that variable as follows.

```
Example:
"variables": {
    "script_path": "{{env `SCRIPT_PATH`}},
}
```

Installing Packer

Let's begin by installing Packer on a Linux virtual machine. In this exercise, we are using the Red Hat OS to install Packer.

Execute the following command to download the Packer package from the HashiCorp website.

```
wget https://releases.hashicorp.com/packer/1.6.6/packer_1.6.6_linux_amd64.zip
```

Execute the following command to extract the Packer binaries (see Figure 6-1).

```
unzip packer_1.6.6_linux_amd64.zip
```

```
[root@inpransb01 packer_directory]# ls
packer_1.6.6_linux_amd64.zip
[root@inpransb01 packer_directory]# unzip packer_1.6.6_linux_amd64.zip
Archive:  packer_1.6.6_linux_amd64.zip
  inflating: packer
```

Figure 6-1. *Extracting Packer binaries*

Execute the following command (first 2 commands) to move the extracted Packer binaries to /usr/bin path (see Figure 6-2) and navigate to /usr/bin path. After installing Packer, verify the installation by executing the second and third commands (see Figure 6-2 and 6-3).

mv packer /usr/bin

cd /usr/bin

Now Run the command to ensure that packer is installed properly. packer

packer -version

```
[root@inpransb01 packer_directory]# packer
Usage: packer [--version] [--help] <command> [<args>]

Available commands are:
    build            build image(s) from template
    console          creates a console for testing variable interpolation
    fix              fixes templates from old versions of packer
    fmt              Rewrites HCL2 config files to canonical format
    hcl2_upgrade     transform a JSON template into an HCL2 configuration
    inspect          see components of a template
    validate         check that a template is valid
    version          Prints the Packer version
```

Figure 6-2. *Verifying Packer*

```
[root@inpransb01 packer_directory]# packer --version
1.6.6
```

Figure 6-3. *Verifying Packer version*

Hands-on Exercise to Automate AWS AMI

Now let's do a hands-on exercise to automate AWS AMI. In this example, we bake a t2.micro AMI using a shell provisioner. We use a shell script for hardening the image using security baselines. After creating the image, we will update it by bundling an application package using Packer. Figure 6-4 shows a high-level flow of the activities performed in this exercise.

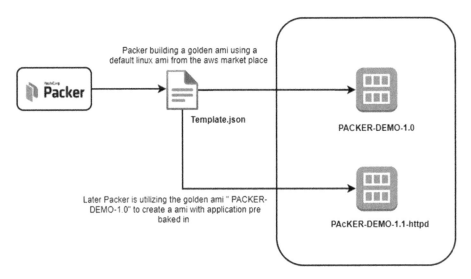

Figure 6-4. *Automating AWS AMI creation using Packer*

Before starting the exercise, ensure that the AWS CLI is installed and configured on the Packer server with the credentials configured for the AWS account created in the previous chapter.

First, set up the AWS CLI tool on the Packer server. Execute the following command to install Python 3.6 on the system.

```
sudo yum install python36
```

Verify the Python version by executing the following command (see Figure 6-5).

```
python3 -version
```

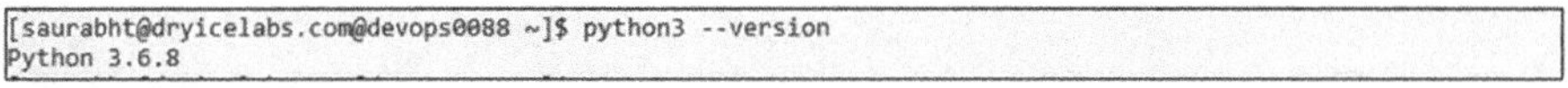

```
[saurabht@dryicelabs.com@devops0088 ~]$ python3 --version
Python 3.6.8
```

Figure 6-5. *AWS CLI tool prerequisite installation*

Install the AWS CLI by executing the following command.

```
pip3 install awscli --upgrade -user
```

Verify the AWS CLI version by executing the following command (see Figure 6-6).

```
aws -version
```

```
[saurabht@dryicelabs.com@devops0088 ~]$ aws --version
aws-cli/1.16.304 Python/3.6.8 Linux/3.10.0-862.el7.x86_64 botocore/1.13.40
[saurabht@dryicelabs.com@devops0088 ~]$
```

Figure 6-6. *AWS CLI tool installation validation*

Configure the AWS account credentials (access and secret key) by executing the following command. Add the secret key, access key (see Chapter 5), and region (eu-west-1). Select JSON as the output format (see Figure 6-7).

```
aws configure
```

```
[saurabht@dryicelabs.com@devops0088 ~]$
[saurabht@dryicelabs.com@devops0088 ~]$ aws configure
AWS Access Key ID [****************YWKP]:
AWS Secret Access Key [****************H64g]:
Default region name [None]: us-east-1
Default output format [None]: json
```

Figure 6-7. *AWS CLI tool configuration*

Execute the following command to set up the Packer project for the hands-on exercise.

mkdir packer_project

Create a script file named server_hardening.sh in the packer_project directory and add the image hardening contents to it. The following are code snippets from the image server baselining script. They are used for regularly checking the integrity of the filesystem.

The following example code is ensuring the integrity of the filesystem.

*sudo echo '0 5 * * * /usr/sbin/aide –check' > /tmp/filenew*
sudo crontab -u root -l | cat - /tmp/filenew | crontab -u root –
sudo rm -rf /tmp/filenew

The following snippet ensures that the SELinux state is set to "Enforcing" and the policy is configured.

Ensure the SELinux state is Enforcing
sudo sed -I '/^SELINUX=/c SELINUX=enforcing' /etc/selinux/
config
Ensure Selinux policy is configured
sudo sed -I '/^SELINUXTYPE=/c SELINUXTYPE=targeted' /etc/
selinux/config

160

The following code snippet triggers security patch installation.

Ensure updates, patches and additional security software are
installed
sudo yum update -security -y

The following code ensures that time synchronization is in use.

sudo yum install ntp -y
sudo echo "restrict -4 default kod nomodify notrap nopeer
noquery" >> /etc/ntp.conf
sudo echo "restrict -6 default kod nomodify notrap nopeer
noquery" >> /etc/ntp.conf

You can download the entire script by cloning it from the following GitHub location and executing the command, as shown in Figure 6-8.

git clone git@github.com:dryice-devops/packer.git

```
[root@inpransb01 packer]# git clone git@github.com:dryice-devops/packer.git
Cloning into 'packer'...

remote: Enumerating objects: 12, done.
remote: Counting objects: 100% (12/12), done.
remote: Compressing objects: 100% (10/10), done.
remote: Total 12 (delta 2), reused 0 (delta 0), pack-reused 0
Receiving objects: 100% (12/12), done.
Resolving deltas: 100% (2/2), done.
[root@inpransb01 packer]#
[root@inpransb01 packer]#
```

Figure 6-8. *Cloning script from GitHub*

The directory created after cloning contains the templates and scripts for our exercise (see Figure 6-9).

```
[root@inpransb01 packer]# cd packer/
[root@inpransb01 packer]# ls
app_script.sh  aws_linux.json  README.md  rhel_hardening.sh
[root@inpransb01 packer]#
```

Figure 6-9. *Reviewing files from GitHub*

Create an aws_ami.json file in the packer_project directory created in the previous step and add content, as shown in Figure 6-11. Copy the cloned server_harderning.sh file to the packer_project directory.

rhel7.8_latest - ami-0881f3111e1e8797b

latest ami pof rhel 7.8 with ansible user created

Root device type: ebs   Virtualization type: hvm   Owner: 711964153936   ENA Enabled: No

Figure 6-10. *Fetching AMI id from AWS Console*

Note   We are using custom AMI (ami-0881f3111e1e8797b) as shown in Figure 6-10, but you can use any RHEL AMI in the marketplace.

Example:

```
{
    "variables": {
        "ami_id": "ami-xxxxxxx",
        },
    "builders": [{
        "type": "amazon-ebs",
        "region": "eu-west-1",
        "source_ami": "{{user `ami_id`}}",
        "instance_type": "t2.micro",
        "ssh_username": "ec2-user",
        "ami_name": "PACKER-DEMO-1.0",
        "tags": {
            "Name": "PACKER-DEMO-1.0",
            "Env": "DEMO"
            }
    }],
```

```
    "provisioners" [
        {
            "type": "shell",
            "script": "server_hardening.sh"
        }
    ]

}
```

```
[root@inpransb01 packer_project]# ls
aws_ami.json  server_hardening.sh
[root@inpransb01 packer_project]# █
```

Figure 6-11. *Packer_project directory content*

Now that the template is ready, the next step will be to execute it for baking the AMI with hardening instructions. Execute the following command to validate the Packer template image. You can inspect the template with the second command (Output shown in Figure 6-12).

```
packer validate aws_ami.json
packer inspect aws_ami.json
```

```
[root@inpransb01 packer_project]# packer validate aws_ami.json
[root@inpransb01 packer_project]# packer inspect aws_ami.json
Packer Inspect: JSON mode
Optional variables and their defaults:

  ami_id = ami-6f68cf0f

Builders:

  amazon-ebs

Provisioners:

  shell

Note: If your build names contain user variables or template
functions such as 'timestamp', these are processed at build time,
and therefore only show in their raw form here.
[root@inpransb01 packer_project]# █
```

Figure 6-12. *Validate and inspect Packer template*

Execute the following command to build the AMI.

packer build aws_ami.json

You can view the AMI by navigating to the EC2 service in AWS Console and clicking AMI (see Figure 6-13).

	Name		AMI Name	▲	AMI ID	▼
	PACKER-DEMO-1.0		packer_linux_a...		ami-0bf84e68a94b25c98	

Figure 6-13. *View AWS AMI using AWS*

Now that we have created the first version of our image, let's perform an exercise to update this image using Packer. Suppose that the AMI we baked in the previous step had an AMI ID, "ami-0bf84e68a94b25c98", from AWS. Let's create a new Packer template called aws_http.json in the packer_project directory, as shown in the following example. Replace the ami_id variable value with the AMI ID created in the AWS account.

Example:

```
{
    "variables": {
        "ami_id": "ami-0bf84e68a94b25c98",
        "app_name": "httpd"
        },
    "builders": [{
        "type": "amazon-ebs",
        "region": "eu-west-1",
        "source_ami": "{{user `ami_id`}}",
        "instance_type": "t2.micro",
        "ssh_username": "ec2-user",
        "ami_name": "PACKER-DEMO-1.1-{{user `app_name` }}",
        "tags": {
            "Name": "PACKER-DEMO-1.0-{{user `app_name` }}",
            "Env": "DEMO"
            }
    }],

    "provisioners" [
        {
            "type": "shell",
            "script": "app_script.sh"
        }
    ]

}
```

Now let's create the app_script.sh script file under the packer_project directory, which includes the steps to install Apache as a package in the image.

```
#!/bin/bash

Sudo yum install apache -y
Sudo systemctl start httpd
Sudo systemctl status httpd
Sudo systemctl enable httpd
```

Before creating a new image using the updated Packer template, let's validate the template by executing the following command.

```
packer validate aws_http.json
```

Note   This command validates the template code (syntax) and returns a zero exit status when successful and a non-zero exit status when a failure.

After successful validation, execute the following command to update AWS AMI with an Apache package in it (see Figure 6-14). Executing the following command validates from AWS.

```
Packer build aws_http.json
```

| PACKER-DEMO-1.0-httpd | packer_linux_a... | ami-0075a3e2911981f8e |

Figure 6-14. *View updated AWS AMI using AWS*

Summary

This chapter covered the main concepts of HashiCorp Packer. You learned how to install open source Packer. You also did a hands-on exercise to create and update AWS AMI.

The next chapter covers the HashiCorp Consul solution and how it manages network access in an application.

CHAPTER 7

Getting Started with HashiCorp Consul

This chapter covers the core concepts of HashiCorp Consul.

- Introduction to HashiCorp Consul

- Installing Consul

- Service discovery using Consul

- DNS and health checks using Consul

Introduction to HashiCorp Consul

HashiCorp Consul provides service discovery, health checks, load balancing, service graph, identity enforcement via TLS, interservice communication, network segmentation, and distributed service configuration management.

The disadvantage with a monolithic application is that if any subcomponents of an application fail, it necessitates redeployment of the entire stack, which is not ideal. The same monolithic app can be delivered as a set of individual, discrete services where the freedom of independently developing and deploying is possible.

© Navin Sabharwal, Sarvesh Pandey and Piyush Pandey 2021
N. Sabharwal et al., *Infrastructure-as-Code Automation Using Terraform, Packer, Vault, Nomad and Consul*, https://doi.org/10.1007/978-1-4842-7129-2_7

However when we move to a microservices architecture there are cross-service challenges, such as service discovery, data consistency, and network communication. Let's look at how Consul helps us to overcome these challenges.

Service Discovery

In a distributed system, the services are on different machines, so the identification/discovery of services is difficult. A load balancer is in front of each service for identification (see Figure 7-1).

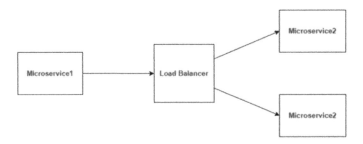

Figure 7-1. *Service discovery*

The disadvantages of service discovery include

- No capability for dynamic auto-discovery/must be managed manually

- Single point of failure

- Communication is through a series of networks and is not direct

Consul overcomes these disadvantages by using a central service registry that contains the entry for all upstream services. The following are some of the advantages of Consul-based service discovery.

- When a service instance starts, it auto-registers on the central registry.

- The service can directly talk to the desired destination service instance without a mediator.

- If one of the service instances or services itself is unhealthy or fails its health check, the registry would then know about this scenario and would avoid returning the service's address; hence, load balancing is also done.

Configuration Management

There is some difficulty in maintaining configurations in a distributed system.

- Maintaining consistency between the configuration on different services after each update is a challenge.

- Dynamically updating a configuration can be a challenge.

Consul overcomes these disadvantages by using a key-value based centralized repository. The entire configuration of all services is stored, which helps with dynamically configuring the services on a distributed system.

Service Mesh and Network Segmentation

A service mesh is an infrastructure layer that handles a high volume of network-based interprocess communication among application services using APIs. It is implemented by a proxy instance, called a *sidecar*, for each service instance.

The following are challenges in a distributed system.

- Controlling the flow of traffic

- Segmenting the network into groups

- Traffic may come from different endpoints and reach different services

- Inability to verify if traffic is from a trusted entity makes security a concern

Consul's solution to these issues is to use

- Service graphs

- Mutual TLS

- Consul Connect

Consul Connect enrolls interservice communication policies and implements them as part of a service graph. For example, a policy might say that service A can talk to service B, but B cannot talk to C. Consul provides a mechanism to enforce such policies without defining firewall rules or IP restrictions using TLS protocol. TLS protocol works based on certificates and these certificates help other services securely identify each other and initiate communication with each other.

Architecture

Consul has good support for multiple datacenters. There is a mixture of clients and servers within each datacenter. Typically, there are three to five servers. However, there is no limit to the number of clients, and they can easily scale into the thousands or tens of thousands. This strikes a balance between performance and availability in the event of failure. Figure 7-2 shows a Consul master server in two datacenters interacting with a Consul client using a gossip protocol.

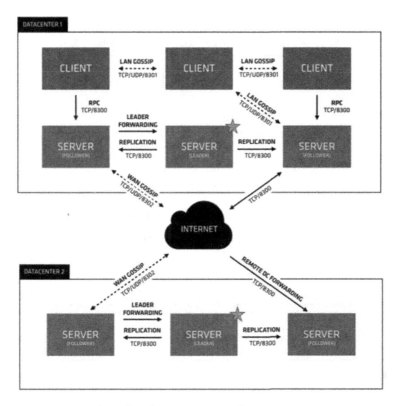

Figure 7-2. *Consul multi-datacenter architecture*

The following describes the key components of Consul.

Agent

An agent is a core component in Consul. It manages and maintains membership information, registers services, and performs checks, like health checks on managed services. The agents are responsible for executing their own health checks and updating their local state. Any agent may run in one of two modes: client or server (see Figure 7-3).

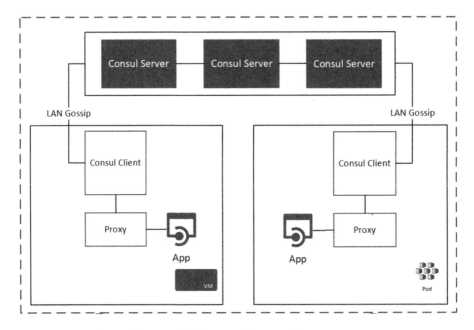

Figure 7-3. *Consul agent (client and server)*

Catalog

Consul leverages a catalog concept for managing all discovered services. It is formed by aggregating the information received from the agents. It can be queried through DNS or HTTP to get information on services (see Figure 7-4).

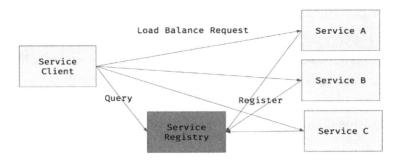

Figure 7-4. *Consul catalog*

Anti-Entropy

Anti-entropy is a mechanism to ensure that running application services are kept stable if any underlying components fail or the system falls into a state of disorder. Consul isolates the global service catalog and the agent's local state. Anti-entropy is a synchronization of the local agent state and the catalog updating the services.

Consensus Protocol

The server-type agents are pooled together under a single raft peer set that works in leader-follower mode. Any transactions received by the follower are forwarded to the leader for processing, and any transactions executed by the leader are replicated to followers. Consul leverages a consensus protocol based on the "Raft: in search of an understandable consensus" algorithm to manage leader-follower interactions.

Raft nodes are always in one of three states: follower, candidate, or leader. A node starts as a follower, promotes to a candidate, and when a quorum of votes are received, becomes a leader.

Gossip Protocol

A gossip protocol is used to broadcast messages within a cluster. The following are the advantages of a gossip protocol.

- There is no need to configure clients with server addresses; discovery is made automatically.

- The work of detecting agent failure is not placed on the servers; it is distributed. It neglects naive heartbeat schemes.

- It is used as a messaging layer to notify when important events, such as leader election, take place.

Consul uses two gossip pools.

LAN Gossip Pool

Each datacenter that Consul operates in has a LAN gossip pool containing all members—clients and servers.

WAN Gossip Pool

All the clusters' servers communicate via a WAN gossip pool. It processes cross-datacenter requests.

Installing Consul

There are three approaches to installing Consul: using a precompiled binary, installing from source, or installing on Kubernetes using a container image. This chapter explains installing Consul using a precompiled binary. To install the precompiled binary, download the appropriate package for your system. (Consul is currently packaged as a zip file.)

This exercise uses a Red Hat virtual machine to install Consul. Make sure that you have Internet access enabled on the virtual machine and the package repo configured to download packages from Red Hat.

Execute the following commands to view the Red Hat OS version. Verify the OS platform type by executing the second command (see Figure 7-5). This value downloads the appropriate package of Consul from the HashiCorp website.

```
cat /etc/redhat-release
uname -m
```

```
[root@ip-10-5-13-156 ~]# cat /etc/redhat-release
Red Hat Enterprise Linux Server release 7.8 (Maipo)
[root@ip-10-5-13-156 ~]# uname -m
x86_64
```

Figure 7-5. *VM OS version verification*

Execute the following command to create a Consul directory. Navigate the directory by executing the second command (see Figure 7-6).

```
mkdir consul
cd consul
```

```
mkdir consul
cd consul
```

Figure 7-6. *Consul directory creation*

Execute the following command to download Consul 1.9.2 package for Linux-based distribution from HashiCorp official website (see Figure 7-7).

```
wget https://releases.hashicorp.com/consul/1.9.2/consul_1.9.2_
linux_amd64.zip
```

```
[root@ip-10-5-13-156 consul]# wget https://releases.hashicorp.com/consul/1.9.2/consul_1.9.2_linux_amd64.zip
--2021-04-01 10:53:07--  https://releases.hashicorp.com/consul/1.9.2/consul_1.9.2_linux_amd64.zip
Resolving releases.hashicorp.com (releases.hashicorp.com)... 151.101.201.183, 2a04:4e42:50::439
Connecting to releases.hashicorp.com (releases.hashicorp.com)|151.101.201.183|:443... connected.
HTTP request sent, awaiting response... 200 OK
Length: 41313084 (39M) [application/zip]
Saving to: 'consul_1.9.2_linux_amd64.zip'

100%[===================================================================================>]

2021-04-01 10:53:08 (91.1 MB/s) - 'consul_1.9.2_linux_amd64.zip' saved [41313084/41313084]
```

Figure 7-7. *Download Consul package*

Execute the first command to extract the Consul package from the zip file. Execute the second command to list extracted files, as shown in Figure 7-8.

```
unzip consul_1.9.2_linux_amd64.zip
```

```
[ansible@ip-10-5-12-84 ~]$ unzip consul_1.9.2_linux_amd64.zip
Archive:  consul_1.9.2_linux_amd64.zip
  inflating: consul
[ansible@ip-10-5-12-84 ~]$ ls
consul   consul_1.9.2_linux_amd64.zip
```

Figure 7-8. *Unzip and list Consul package*

Execute the following command to move Consul binary to /usr/bin location to invoke Consul commands without modifying the PATH variable.

```
mv consul /usr/bin/
```

Execute the following command to verify installation of Consul, as shown in Figure 7-9.

```
consul --version
```

```
[root@consul consul]# consul --version
Consul v1.9.2
Revision 6530cf370
Protocol 2 spoken by default, understands 2 to 3 (agent will automatically use protocol >2 when speaking to com
patible agents)
```

Figure 7-9. *Consul installation verification*

Execute the following command to start the Consul agent in development mode, as shown in Figure 7-10.

```
consul agent –dev –ui –bind '{{ GetInterfaceIP "eth0" }}' –
client 0.0.0.0
```

```
[ansible@ip-10-5-12-84 ~]$ consul agent -dev -ui -bind '{{ GetInterfaceIP "eth0" }}' -client 0.0.0.0
==> Starting Consul agent...
           Version: '1.9.2'
           Node ID: 'dddf6a81-f79b-a3ee-9155-15537c5e2470'
         Node name: 'ip-10-5-12-84'
        Datacenter: 'dc1' (Segment: '<all>')
            Server: true (Bootstrap: false)
       Client Addr: [0.0.0.0] (HTTP: 8500, HTTPS: -1, gRPC: 8502, DNS: 8600)
      Cluster Addr: 10.5.12.84 (LAN: 8301, WAN: 8302)
           Encrypt: Gossip: false, TLS-Outgoing: false, TLS-Incoming: false, Auto-Encrypt-TLS: false

==> Log data will now stream in as it occurs:
```

Figure 7-10. *Consul agent setup*

Execute the following commands to query the Consul leader and peers, as shown in Figure 7-11.

```
curl http://127.0.0.1:8500/v1/status/leader
curl http://127.0.0.1:8500/v1/status/peers
```

```
[ansible@ip-10-5-12-84 ~]$ curl http://127.0.0.1:8500/v1/status/leader
"10.5.12.84:8300"
[ansible@ip-10-5-12-84 ~]$ curl http://127.0.0.1:8500/v1/status/peers
[
    "10.5.12.84:8300"
]
[ansible@ip-10-5-12-84 ~]$ ▊
```

Figure 7-11. *Query Consul leader and peers*

Execute the following commands to see the Consul members, as shown in Figure 7-12.

```
consul members
```

```
[ansible@ip-10-5-12-84 ~]$ consul members
Node            Address          Status  Type    Build  Protocol  DC   Segment
ip-10-5-12-84   10.5.12.84:8301  alive   server  1.9.2  2         dc1  <all>
[ansible@ip-10-5-12-84 ~]$ ▊
```

Figure 7-12. *View Consul members*

Service Discovery Using Consul

The main goal of service discovery is to provide a catalog of available services. A service can be associated with a health check.

A service definition can have either a .json or .hcl extension or registered dynamically using the HTTP API. The following are things to keep in mind when using service definitions in Consul.

- A service definition must include a name and may include an ID, tags, address, meta, port, enable_tag_ override, and check.

- A service can have an associated health check to remove failing nodes.

- Proxies used with Connect are registered as services in Consul's catalog.

- Services may contain a token field to provide an ACL token.

- The connect field can be specified to configure Connect for a service. This field is available in Consul 1.2.0 and later.

- Multiple services definitions can be provided at once using the plural services key in your configuration file.

Now let's look at a typical service definition file, as shown in Listings 7-1 and 7-2. The following samples are the service definitions for two services: dashboard and counting. Both services have defined the health check mechanism (i.e., HTTP-based and port to be used).

Listing 7-1. Sample Dashboard Service Definition File

```
service {
name = "dashboard"
port = 9002

connect {
sidecar_service {
proxy {
upstreams = [
{
destination_name = "counting"
local_bind_port = 5000
}
]
}
}
}
check {
id = "dashboard-check"
http = "http://localhost:9002/health"
method = "GET"
interval = "1s"
timeout = "1s"
}
}
```

Listing 7-2. Sample Counting Service Definition File

```
service {
name = "counting"
id = "counting-1"
port = 9003
```

```
connect {
sidecar_service {}
}
check {
id = "counting-check"
http = "http://localhost:9003/health"
method = "GET"
interval = "1s"
timeout = "1s"
}
}
```

There are several ways to register services in Consul.

- Directly from a Consul-aware application

- From an orchestrator, like Nomad or Kubernetes

- Using configuration files that are loaded at node startup

- Using the API to register them with a JSON or HCL specification

- Using the CLI to simplify this submission process

Let's start with a hands-on exercise that registers the dashboard and counting services on the Consul server using CLI.

Create a directory called Test and navigate within it. Execute the command in Listing 7-3 to clone the sample template files from GitHub, and then execute the next command to unzip the two files for the dashboard and counting services.

Listing 7-3. Cloning and Unzipping the Binaries

```
git clone git@github.com:dryice-devops/consul.git
unzip counting-service_linux_amd64.zip
unzip dashboard-service_linux_amd64.zip
```

Execute the following commands to set up the dashboard and counting services in listening mode on the Consul server, as shown in Figures 7-13 and 7-14.

```
PORT=9002 COUNTING_SERVICE_URL="http://localhost:5000" ./
dashboard-service_linux_amd64 &
PORT=9003 ./counting-service_linux_amd64 &
```

```
[root@consul consul]# PORT=9002 COUNTING_SERVICE_URL="http://localhost:5000" ./dashboard-service_linux_amd64 &
[1] 8614
[root@consul consul]# Starting server on http://0.0.0.0:9002
(Pass as PORT environment variable)
Using counting service at http://localhost:5000
(Pass as COUNTING_SERVICE_URL environment variable)
Starting websocket server...
```

Figure 7-13. *Starting dashboard service*

```
[root@consul consul]# PORT=9003 ./counting-service_linux_amd64 &
[4] 13983
[root@consul consul]# Serving at http://localhost:9003
(Pass as PORT environment variable)
```

Figure 7-14. *Starting counting service*

Execute the following commands to register the dashboard and counting services with Consul, as shown in Figure 7-15. Make sure that you have created the counting and dashboard files, as shown in Figures 7-16 and 7-17.

```
consul services register counting.hcl
consul services register dashboard.hcl
```

```
[root@ip-10-5-12-84 test]# consul services register counting.hcl
Registered service: counting
[root@ip-10-5-12-84 test]# consul services register dashboard.hcl
Registered service: dashboard
[root@ip-10-5-12-84 test]#
```

Figure 7-15. *Registering services in Consul*

Execute the following command to verify that the services registered successfully in Consul, as shown in Figure 7-16.

```
consul catalog services
```

```
[root@ip-10-5-12-84 consul_dir]# consul catalog services
consul
counting
counting-sidecar-proxy
dashboard
dashboard-sidecar-proxy
[root@ip-10-5-12-84 consul_dir]#
```

Figure 7-16. *Verifying service registration*

Execute the following command to create an intention for the counting and dashboard services (see Figure 7-17). Intentions define access control for services in the service mesh and control which services may establish connections. The default intention behavior for dev agents is defined by the default ACL policy, which is "allow all".

```
consul intention create dashboard counting
```

```
[root@ip-10-5-12-84 ~]# consul intention create dashboard counting
Created: dashboard => counting (allow)
[root@ip-10-5-12-84 ~]# consul intention create -deny -replace dashboard counting
[root@ip-10-5-12-84 ~]#
```

Figure 7-17. *Intention creation using Consul*

Execute the following commands to start the built-in sidecar proxy for the counting and dashboard services, as shown in Figures 7-18 and 7-19.

```
consul connect proxy -sidecar-for counting-1 > counting-proxy.
log &
consul connect proxy -sidecar-for dashboard > dashboard-proxy.
log &
```

```
[root@consul consul]# consul connect proxy -sidecar-for counting-1 > counting-proxy.log &
[2] 9954
```

Figure 7-18. *Starting sidecar proxy for counting service*

```
[root@consul consul]# consul connect proxy -sidecar-for dashboard > dashboard-proxy.log &
[3] 10306
```

Figure 7-19. *Starting sidecar proxy for dashboard service*

You can verify the service registration by opening the Consul UI. Navigate to http://<IP of your Consul Server>:8500/ui to open the Consul UI in your browser (see Figure 7-20). Click the Services tab to view the registered services list.

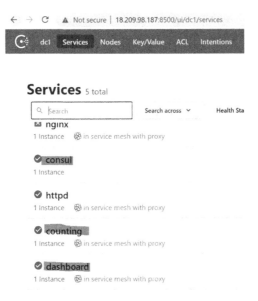

Figure 7-20. *Consul UI*

Click the counting service to see the registered service information, as shown in Figure 7-21.

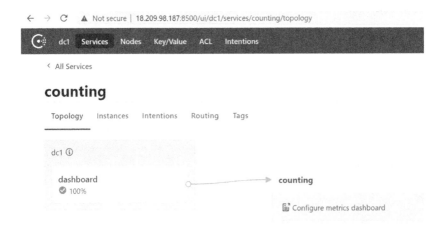

Figure 7-21. *Counting Service navigation on Consul UI*

Navigate to http://<IP of your Consul Server>:9002 to access the
Dashboard service, as shown in Figure 7-22.

Figure 7-22. *Dashboard service browser navigation*

A positive number on the screen indicates that a connection between
the services has been established. This number indicates the amount of
time (in seconds) the user has been connected to the front-end portal.
Also, the green Connected status in the top-right corner indicates a
successful connection.

Intention Deletion

Now let's try to disrupt the service connectivity between the counting and
dashboard services by deleting the intention.

Execute the following command to delete the intention, as shown in
Figure 7-23.

```
consul intention delete dashboard counting
```

```
[root@ip-10-5-12-84 ~]# consul intention delete dashboard counting
Intention deleted.
[root@ip-10-5-12-84 ~]#
```

Figure 7-23. *Deleting intention*

To test whether traffic is flowing through the sidecar proxies, let's create a deny intention by executing the following command.

```
consul intention create -deny -replace dashboard counting
```

Navigate to http://<IP of your Consul Server>:9002 to access the dashboard service, as shown in Figure 7-24.

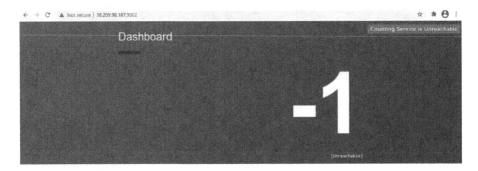

Figure 7-24. Connection lost

The negative number and the "Counting Service is Unreachable" message in the top corner indicate that the connectivity between the services is lost.

Execute the following command to restore communication between the services by replacing the deny intention with an allow (see Figure 7-25).

```
consul intention create -allow -replace dashboard counting
```

```
[root@ip-10-5-12-84 test]# consul intention create -allow -replace dashboard counting
[root@ip-10-5-12-84 test]# Fetched count 62
```

Figure 7-25. Allow intention creation

You can validate the connection restore by navigating back to the Dashboard service page, as shown in Figure 7-26.

Figure 7-26. *Connection restored*

Now let's look at another example of managing communication between two applications. The LAMP stack and Nginx demonstrate Consul's capabilities in managing communication. Let's start with the installation of the LAMP stack and Nginx. We will enable Apache and Nginx as services on Consul and then manage the communication between them.

Execute the following command to install an HTTPd package, and then enable service to start up on reboot, as shown in Figure 7-27.

```
yum install httpd
systemctl enable httpd.service
```

```
[root@ip-10-5-13-156 consul]#
[root@ip-10-5-13-156 consul]# yum install httpd
Loaded plugins: amazon-id, search-disabled-repos
Resolving Dependencies
--> Running transaction check
---> Package httpd.x86_64 0:2.4.6-97.el7_9 will be installed
--> Processing Dependency: httpd-tools = 2.4.6-97.el7_9 for package: httpd-2.4.6-97.el7_9.x86_64
--> Processing Dependency: /etc/mime.types for package: httpd-2.4.6-97.el7_9.x86_64
--> Processing Dependency: libaprutil-1.so.0()(64bit) for package: httpd-2.4.6-97.el7_9.x86_64
--> Processing Dependency: libapr-1.so.0()(64bit) for package: httpd-2.4.6-97.el7_9.x86_64
--> Running transaction check
---> Package apr.x86_64 0:1.4.8-7.el7 will be installed
---> Package apr-util.x86_64 0:1.5.2-6.el7 will be installed
---> Package httpd-tools.x86_64 0:2.4.6-97.el7_9 will be installed
---> Package mailcap.noarch 0:2.1.41-2.el7 will be installed
--> Finished Dependency Resolution

Dependencies Resolved
```

Figure 7-27. *Installing Apache*

Execute the following command to start the Apache service.

```
systemctl start httpd.service
```

Execute the following command to install the MySQL package, and then enable the service to start up on reboot, as shown in Figure 7-28.

```
yum install mysql-server mysql
systemctl enable mysqld.service
```

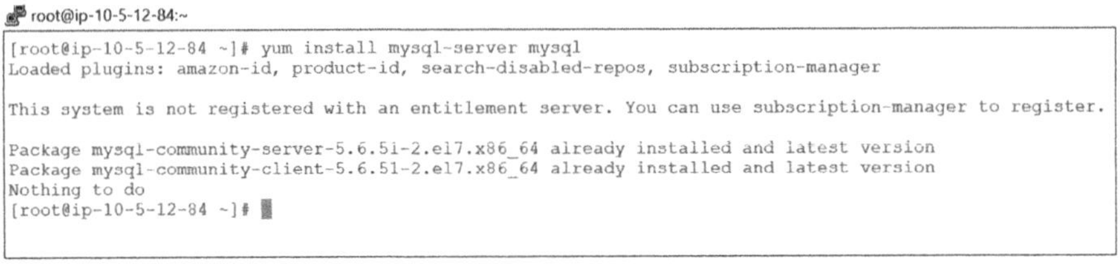

```
 root@ip-10-5-12-84:~
[root@ip-10-5-12-84 ~]# yum install mysql-server mysql
Loaded plugins: amazon-id, product-id, search-disabled-repos, subscription-manager

This system is not registered with an entitlement server. You can use subscription-manager to register.

Package mysql-community-server-5.6.51-2.el7.x86_64 already installed and latest version
Package mysql-community-client-5.6.51-2.el7.x86_64 already installed and latest version
Nothing to do
[root@ip-10-5-12-84 ~]#
```

Figure 7-28. *Installation of MySQL*

Execute the following command to start the MySQL service.

```
systemctl start mysqld.service
```

Execute the following command to configure MySQL to remove anonymous users and other default tables and provide the input shown in Figures 7-29 and 7-30.

```
mysql_secure_installation
```

```
[root@ip-10-5-12-84 ~]# mysql_secure_installation


NOTE: RUNNING ALL PARTS OF THIS SCRIPT IS RECOMMENDED FOR ALL MySQL
      SERVERS IN PRODUCTION USE!  PLEASE READ EACH STEP CAREFULLY!

In order to log into MySQL to secure it, we'll need the current
password for the root user.  If you've just installed MySQL, and
you haven't set the root password yet, the password will be blank,
so you should just press enter here.

Enter current password for root (enter for none):
OK, successfully used password, moving on...

Setting the root password ensures that nobody can log into the MySQL
root user without the proper authorisation.

You already have a root password set, so you can safely answer 'n'.

Change the root password? [Y/n] n
 ... skipping.

By default, a MySQL installation has an anonymous user, allowing anyone
to log into MySQL without having to have a user account created for
them.  This is intended only for testing, and to make the installation
go a bit smoother.  You should remove them before moving into a
production environment.

Remove anonymous users? [Y/n] Y
 ... Success!

Normally, root should only be allowed to connect from 'localhost'.  This
ensures that someone cannot guess at the root password from the network.

Disallow root login remotely? [Y/n] Y
 ... Success!

By default, MySQL comes with a database named 'test' that anyone can
access.  This is also intended only for testing, and should be removed
before moving into a production environment.

Remove test database and access to it? [Y/n] Y
```

Figure 7-29. *Reconfiguring MySQL*

```
Remove test database and access to it? [Y/n] Y
 - Dropping test database...
ERROR 1008 (HY000) at line 1: Can't drop database 'test'; database doesn't exist
 ... Failed!  Not critical, keep moving...
 - Removing privileges on test database...
 ... Success!

Reloading the privilege tables will ensure that all changes made so far
will take effect immediately.

Reload privilege tables now? [Y/n] Y
 ... Success!



All done!  If you've completed all of the above steps, your MySQL
installation should now be secure.

Thanks for using MySQL!

Cleaning up...
```

Figure 7-30. *Reconfiguring MySQL*

Execute the following command to install the PHP package.

```
yum -y install php php-mysqlnd php-cli
```

Execute the following command to restart the Apache service.

```
systemctl restart httpd.service
```

Create a basic PHP configuration with the basic content shown next by creating a test.php file under the/var/www/html directory.

```
<?php phpinfo(); ?>
```

Access the test.php file created in the previous step by navigating to http://<IP address of your Consul server>/test.php, as shown in Figure 7-31.

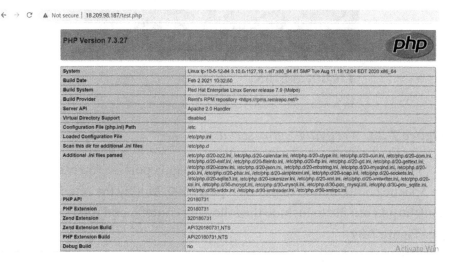

Figure 7-31. *Accessing Test.php file*

Execute the following command to install Nginx and enable the service to start up at reboot, as shown in Figure 7-32.

```
yum install nginx
systemctl enable nginx
```

```
[root@consul consul]# yum install nginx
Loaded plugins: amazon-id, search-disabled-repos
Package 1:nginx-1.17.5-9334.el7.art.x86_64 already installed and latest version
Nothing to do
```

Figure 7-32. *Installation of Nginx*

Execute the following command to start the Nginx service.

```
systemctl start nginx
```

You can also verify the default Nginx installation by accessing http://< IP address of your Consul server> (see Figure 7-33).

191

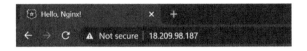

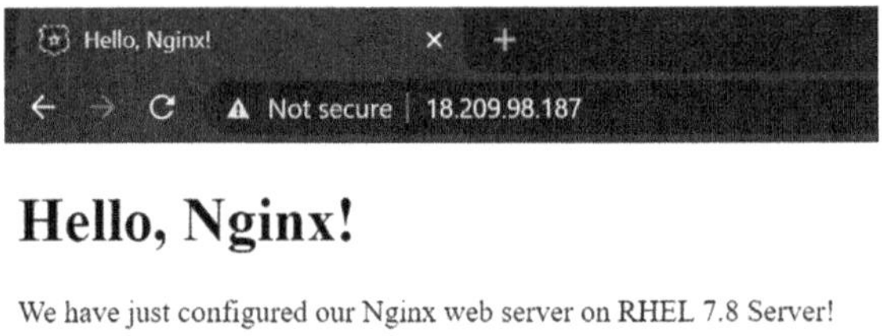

Hello, Nginx!
Not secure | 18.209.98.187
Hello, Nginx!
We have just configured our Nginx web server on RHEL 7.8 Server!

Figure 7-33. *Verifying Nginx service*

The Apache port may conflict with the Nginx port, so you can modify an Apache configuration to listen on port 8080. Modify the /etc/httpd/conf/httpd.conf file to include the following content, and then save the file (see Figure 7-34).

```
Listen 127.0.0.1:8080
```

```
[root@ip-10-5-12-84 ~]# cat /etc/httpd/conf/httpd.conf  | grep Listen
# Listen: Allows you to bind Apache to specific IP addresses and/or
# Change this to Listen on specific IP addresses as shown below to
#Listen 12.34.56.78:80
Listen 127.0.0.1:8080
[root@ip-10-5-12-84 ~]#
```

Figure 7-34. *Updating Apache listing port*

Also modify the document root in the /usr/share/nginx/html file, as shown in Figure 7-35.

```
DocumentRoot "/usr/share/nginx/html/"
```

```
[root@ip-10-5-12-84 ~]# cat /etc/httpd/conf/httpd.conf  | grep DocumentRoot
# DocumentRoot: The directory out of which you will serve your
DocumentRoot "/usr/share/nginx/html"
    # access content that does not live under the DocumentRoot.
[root@ip-10-5-12-84 ~]#
```

Figure 7-35. *Updating document root*

Execute the following command to restart the Apache service.

```
systemctl restart httpd.service
```

Make sure the Nginx configuration file can process the PHP locations, as shown in Listing 7-4.

Listing 7-4. Nginx Configuration File

```
server {
listen 80;
root /usr/share/nginx/html;
index index.php index.htm index.html;
server_name _;

location / {
try_files $uri $uri/ /index.php;
}

location ~ \.php$ {
proxy_pass http://127.0.0.1:8080;
proxy_set_header Host $host;
proxy_set_header X-Real-IP $remote_addr;
proxy_set_header X-Forwarded-For $remote_addr;
}

location ~ /\.ht {
deny all;
}
```

Service Registration

Let's register the Nginx and LAMP services. Create nginx.hcl and apache. hcl files, as shown in Listings 7-5 and 7-6.

Listing 7-5. Nginx Configuration File

```
service {
name = "nginx"
id = "nginx"
port = 80
address = "10.5.12.84"

tags = ["webfrontend"]
meta = {
version = "1"
}

check {
id = "nginx url hit"
http = "http://10.5.12.84:80"
method = "GET"
interval = "1s"
timeout = "1s"
}
}
```

Listing 7-6. Apache Configuration File

```
service {
name = "apache"
id = "apache"
port = 8080
address = "127.0.0.1"
tags = ["httpd"]
meta = {
version = "1"
}
```

```
check {
id = "apache url hit"
http = "http://10.5.12.84:8080"
method = "GET"
interval = "1s"
timeout = "1s"
}
}
```

Execute the following commands to register Nginx and Apache services with Consul.

```
consul services register nginx.hcl
consul services register apache.hcl
```

Execute the following command to create intention for the Apache and Nginx service.

```
consul intention create apache nginx
```

Log in to the Consul UI (http://<IP Address of your Consul server>:8500/ui) and navigate to the Service tab to view both the Apache and Nginx services, as shown in Figure 7-36.

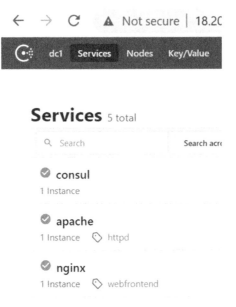

Figure 7-36. *Review Apache and Nginx service on Consul GUI*

Click each service to view the details.

Check Nginx's health status. The status is 200 OK, if the health check has passed (i.e., web page is reachable as per our health check definition). The default health check verifies that the node is alive, reachable, and has passed (see Figure 7-37).

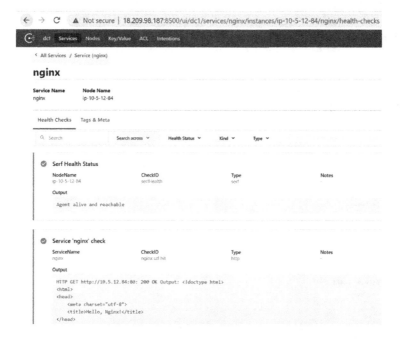

Figure 7-37. *Review Nginx service on Consul GUI*

Check Apache's health status. The status is 200 OK, if the health check has passed. The default health check determines if the node is alive, reachable, and has passed (see Figure 7-38).

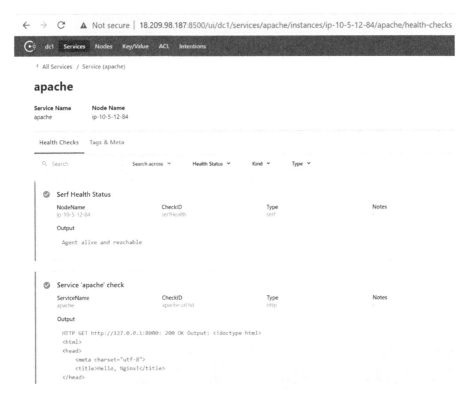

Figure 7-38. *Review Apache service on Consul GUI*

DNS and Health Checks Using Consul

The DNS, without any high integration with Consul, allows applications to use service discovery. By default, Consul listens on 127.0.0.1:8600 for DNS queries. nslookup or dig tools can interact with a DNS server.

```
Dig @127.0.0.1 -p 8600 redis.service.dc1.consul. ANY
```

From a Windows OS perspective, nslookup should be used. From a Linux OS perspective, dig can be used in addition to nslookup. Make sure the bind-utils package is present for dig usage in a Linux environment.

A health check is application-specific; if not integrated, it has a scope at the node level.

There are several different types of checks.

- **HTTP checks** make an HTTP GET request to the specified URL.

- **TCP checks** make a TCP connection attempt to the specified IP/hostname and port.

- **TTL checks** retain their last known state for a given TTL. The state of the check must be updated periodically over the HTTP interface.

- **Docker checks** invoke an external application that is packaged within a Docker container.

- **gRPC checks** the whole application. Checks are intended for applications that support the standard gRPC health-checking protocol.

- **Alias checks** are for a local service. They check the health state of another registered node or service.

Summary

This chapter covered in detail the main concepts of HashiCorp Consul. We learned how to install open source Consul and also performed a hands-on exercise involving application service discovery using Consul.

The next chapter covers the HashiCorp Nomad solution and how it can be used to manage the orchestration of containerized and non-containerized applications.

CHAPTER 8

Getting Started with Nomad

This chapter discusses the core concepts of HashiCorp Nomad. You should have a basic understanding of container orchestration, scheduling, and autoscaling functionalities. The chapter covers the following topics.

- Container orchestration

- Introduction to Nomad

- Installing Nomad

- Policy-driven governance using Nomad

- Container application deployment using Nomad

Container Orchestration

Containers are a way to wrap up an application into its own isolated package. Everything the application requires to run successfully as a process is captured and executed within the container. A container enables bundling all application dependencies, such as library dependencies and runtimes. This enables standardization and consistency across environments because the container comes preloaded with all the prerequisite/dependencies required to run the application service.

© Navin Sabharwal, Sarvesh Pandey and Piyush Pandey 2021
N. Sabharwal et al., *Infrastructure-as-Code Automation Using Terraform, Packer, Vault, Nomad and Consul*, https://doi.org/10.1007/978-1-4842-7129-2_8

You can develop the application code on your personal workstation and then safely deploy it to run in production-level infrastructure.

A container is an instance of a container image. A container image is a way to package an app or service (like a snapshot) and then deploy it in a reliable and reproducible way (see Figure 8-1).

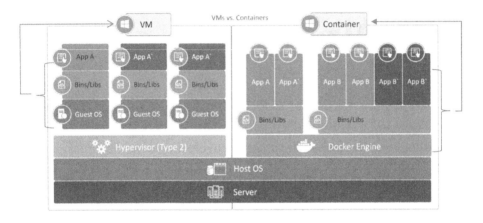

Figure 8-1. *Container vs. VM comparison*

Building applications using containers brings agility to developing, testing, and deploying any application across any cloud. With containers, you can take any app from development to production with little or no code change. You can use a manual approach or use a CI/CD tool with IaC solutions to deploy your application code. You might need to perform tasks like modifying configuration items, copying application content between servers, and running interactive setup programs based on application setups, followed by testing. In a manual setup, this can consume significant time.

What if you have many applications to manage? Managing each one of them manually is very time-consuming. You need to create and destroy hundreds of containers and monitor each one of them. If a container encounters an error, which could cause the downtime of critical applications, you'd need to destroy and provision a new one. Even worse, what if your thousands of containers were scattered across hundreds of servers? You need to keep track of which server contains which containers and which application each container belongs to.

Container orchestration has been introduced to overcome the manual effort of managing containers. It helps minimize the hassle of provisioning, destroying, controlling, and scaling containers.

Container orchestration tools provide a framework for managing containers and microservices architecture at scale. Nomad is a container orchestration tool for container lifecycle management. Nomad orchestration allows you to build application services that can span across multiple containers, schedule containers across a cluster, and manage their health over time.

Nomad eliminates most of the manual intervention involved in deploying and scaling containerized applications. Nomad can cluster groups of hosts on physical or virtual machines and run Linux containers. Nomad offers a platform to easily and efficiently manage clusters.

In the Nomad container orchestration tool, HCL describes the configuration of an application. The configuration file tells the configuration management tool to find the container images, establish a network, and store logs.

When deploying a new container, Nomad automatically schedules a deployment to a cluster and finds the right host, considering any defined requirements or restrictions. It then manages the container's lifecycle based on the specifications.

Container orchestration can be used in any environment that runs containers, including on-premise servers and public or private cloud environments.

Introduction to Nomad

Nomad has a built-in feature to deploy/upgrade applications using blue/ green and canary deployments.

Nomad can integrate with HashiCorp Terraform, Consul, and Vault. It is suited for easy integration into an organization's existing workflows. It comes in two versions Open Source and Enterprise, the following Table 8-1 lists the differences between the two.

Table 8-1. *Nomad: Open Source vs. Enterprise*

Nomad Features	Open Source	Enterprise
Service and Batch Scheduling	✓	✓
Task Drivers	✓	✓
Device Plug-ins	✓	✓
Multi-Upgrade Strategies	✓	✓
Federation	✓	✓
Autoscaling	✓	✓
Container Storage Interface plug-in	✓	✓
Container Network Interface plug-in	✓	✓
Access Control System	✓	✓
Web UI	✓	✓
Consul Integration	✓	✓
Vault Integration	✓	✓
Namespaces	✓	✓
ENTERPRISE PLATFORM	X	✓
Automated Upgrades	X	✓

(*continued*)

Table 8-1. (*continued*)

Nomad Features	Open Source	Enterprise
Automated Backup	X	✓
Enhanced Read Scalability	X	✓
Redundancy Zones	X	✓
Multi-Vault Namespaces	X	✓

The following describes Nomad's key features.

- **Service and batch scheduling**: Nomad provides service and batch scheduling. It can restart or reschedule jobs.

- **Task driver support for multiple platforms**: Task drivers in Nomad are runtime components that execute workloads. The task drivers support Docker, Java, and binaries running on the host operating system.

- **Multi-device plug-ins**: Detects and makes devices available to tasks in Nomad. Devices are physical hardware that exist on a node, such as a GPU or an FPGA. By having extensible device plug-ins, Nomad has the flexibility to support a broad set of devices and allows the community to build additional device plug-ins as needed.

- **Multiple upgrade strategies**: Most applications are long-lived and require updates over time. Nomad has built-in support for rolling, blue/green, and canary updates to deploy a new application or upgrade to a new version of the application. When a job specifies a rolling update, Nomad uses task state and health check information to detect allocation health and minimize or eliminate downtime.

- **Multi-region federation**: This built-in capability allows multiple clusters to be linked together.

- **Autoscaling**: The Nomad autoscaler periodically checks for jobs with queued allocations, ensuring enough capacity to schedule these allocations. Whenever there isn't enough capacity, a scale-up event is triggered.

- **Container storage interface plug-in**: Manages external storage volumes for stateful workloads running inside your cluster. CSI providers are third-party plug-ins that run as jobs and can mount volumes created by your cloud provider. Nomad is aware of CSI-managed volumes during the scheduling process, enabling it to schedule your workloads based on the availability of volumes from a specific client.

- **Container network interface plug-in**: Supports CNI plug-ins while deploying on containerized applications.

- **Access control system**: Enables access of policies and tokens to only authorized users and applications.

- **Consul integration**: Enables automatic clustering, built-in service registration, and dynamic rendering of configuration files and environment variables.

- **Vault integration**: Nomad integrates with HashiCorp Vault to enable secure, auditable, and easy access to your secrets.

- **Namespaces**: Supports namespaces, allowing jobs and their associated objects to be segmented from each other and other cluster users.

- **Sentinel**: Sentinel is a language and framework for building policies. This feature is available in the Enterprise version. A Sentinel policy describes the allowed actions under specific scenarios or conditions. Sentinel integration builds on the ACL system. It provides the ability to create fine-grained policy enforcement.

Nomad Architecture

The Nomad architecture shown in Figure 8-2 consists of client and server components within the same region. Servers in a region act as the brain of the cluster and are used for managing jobs, clients, and deployments, including aspects like resource placement decisions. Each region may have clients from multiple datacenters, allowing a small number of servers to handle very large clusters.

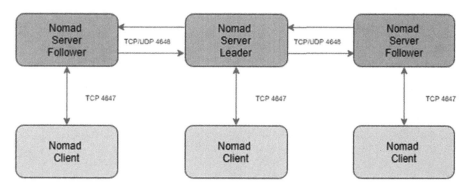

Figure 8-2. *Single region Nomad architecture*

Nomad servers always have leader-follower relationships. They use a consensus protocol based on the Raft algorithm for state replication. Nomad servers in every region are all part of a single consensus group. This means that they work together to elect a single leader, which has extra duties. The leader is responsible for processing all queries and transactions.

Nomad execution is concurrent, meaning all servers participate in making scheduling decisions in parallel. The leader provides the additional coordination necessary to do this safely and to ensure clients are not oversubscribed.

The servers create tasks from the jobs provided by the end user. The servers send them across to the clients where those jobs are executed.

The agent running on the client is responsible for registering with the servers, watching for any work to be assigned, and executing tasks. The Nomad agent is a long-lived process that interfaces with the servers.

When providing availability or scalability, Nomad may be in a multi-region setup (see Figure 8-3). This topology helps the user to interact with Nomad servers in any region.

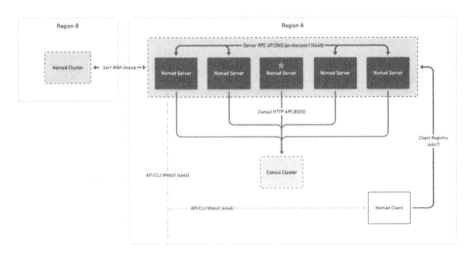

Figure 8-3. *Multi-region Nomad architecture*

Nomad server clusters in different datacenters can be federated using WAN links. The server clusters can be joined to communicate over the WAN on port 4648. This same port is used for single datacenter deployments over LAN.

Servers within two regions are loosely coupled and communicate using a gossip protocol, which allows users to submit jobs to any region or query the state of any region transparently. Requests are forwarded to the appropriate server to be processed, and the results are returned.

Let's look at key concepts or terminologies that are used while working with Nomad.

- **Nomad agent/client**: A Nomad agent is a long-running process that runs on every machine that is part of the Nomad cluster. It works in either server mode or client mode (depending on the server where an agent is running). Clients are responsible for running tasks, whereas servers are responsible for managing the cluster.

- **Nomad follower**: All nodes start as followers and can accept log entries from a leader, cast votes, and receive health checks, heartbeat, and liveness for all the nodes.

- **Nomad leader**: The peer set elects a single node to be the leader whenever it wants. The leader ingests new log entries, replicates to followers, and manages committed entries.

- **Job**: A task submitted by the user is called a *job* in Nomad. It contains instructions that determine what should be done but not where it should be run. Nomad makes sure the final state (after a job is completed) matches the user's desired state. A job is composed of one or more task groups.

- **Task group**: Multiple sets of tasks that must be run together in a job. It is the scheduling unit, meaning the entire group must run on the same client node and not be split.

- **Driver**: Represents the basic means of executing your Tasks. Binary files, Docker, and Java, are examples of drivers.

- **Task**: A task is the smallest unit of work in Nomad. Tasks are dependent on browsers, which allow Nomad to be flexible in the types of tasks it supports.

- **Client**: Refers to the workloads where tasks are executed.

- **Allocation**: A mapping between a task group in a job and a client node. Nomad servers create them as part of scheduling during an evaluation.

- **Bin packing**: The process that maximizes the utilization of bins. In Nomad, the clients are bins, and the items are task groups.

Autoscaling Overview

When a job is launched in Nomad, the master scheduler tries to find available capacity to run it. In cases where there are not enough resources to meet the job's demands, queued allocations and metrics show that the job cannot run due to exhausted nodes. In such scenarios, Nomad supports the following autoscaling mechanisms to overcome resource issues.

Dynamic Application Sizing

Dynamic Application Sizing enables organizations to optimize the resource consumption of applications using sizing recommendations. It evaluates, processes, and stores historical task resource usage data, making recommendations on CPU and memory resource parameters. The recommendations can be calculated using several different algorithms to ensure the best fit for the application.

Dynamic Application Sizing can be enabled on an individual task by configuring autoscaling policies within the task stanza using the job specification scaling block.

Horizontal Cluster Autoscaling

Horizontal cluster autoscaling adds or removes Nomad clients from a cluster to ensure there is an appropriate cluster resource for the scheduled applications. Cluster scaling is enabled by configuring the autoscaler agent with policies targeting the Nomad cluster.

Horizontal Application Autoscaling

Horizontal application autoscaling automatically controls the number of instances to have sufficient work throughput to meet service-level agreements (SLAs). In Nomad, horizontal application autoscaling modifies the number of allocations in a task group based on the value of a relevant metric, such as CPU and memory utilization or the number of open connections.

Installing Nomad

Let's begin with a hands-on exercise to install a Nomad server and client. A cluster in any type of topology in Nomad (single region or multi-region) typically consists of three to five servers and a few client agents. Nomad divides the whole infrastructure into regions that can be under one server cluster. It can manage multiple datacenters or availability zones. This exercise is a three-node Nomad setup with one node client on an AWS EC2 machine. We use four servers with two CPUs and 8 GB RAM on an Amazon Linux operating system.

First, create four EC2 instances on AWS with an Amazon Linux OS and ensure the servers can communicate with each other without any restrictions from the security group. Also, ensure you have Internet access available on the virtual machine to download the package.

Execute the following command to clone the code used in this chapter, as shown in Figure 8-4.

```
git clone https://github.com/dryice-devops/nomad.git
```

```
[root@ip-10-5-12-43 repo]# git clone https://github.com/dryice-devops/nomad.git
Cloning into 'nomad'...
remote: Enumerating objects: 21, done.
remote: Counting objects: 100% (21/21), done.
remote: Compressing objects: 100% (17/17), done.
remote: Total 21 (delta 4), reused 0 (delta 0), pack-reused 0
Unpacking objects: 100% (21/21), done.
[root@ip-10-5-12-43 repo]#
```

Figure 8-4. *Cloning lab files from GitHub*

Execute the following command to export the Nomad_Version variable value, as shown in Figure 8-5.

```
export NOMAD_VERSION="1.0.1"
```

```
[root@ip-172-31-38-249 ~]# export NOMAD_VERSION="1.0.1"
[root@ip-172-31-38-249 ~]#
```

Figure 8-5. *Exporting environment variable*

Execute the following command to download the precompiled binary, as shown in Figure 8-6.

```
curl –silent --remote-name https://releases.hashicorp.com/
nomad/${NOMAD_VERSION}/nomad_${NOMAD_VERSION}_linux_amd64.zip
```

```
[root@ip-172-31-38-249 ~]# curl --silent --remote-name https://releases.hashicorp.com/nomad/${NOMAD
_VERSION}/nomad_${NOMAD_VERSION}_linux_amd64.zip
[root@ip-172-31-38-249 ~]# ls -lrt --color=never
total 38520
-rw-r--r-- 1 root root 39444296 Mar  8 00:58 nomad_1.0.1_linux_amd64.zip
[root@ip-172-31-38-249 ~]#
```

Figure 8-6. *Downloading precompiled Nomad binary*

Execute the following commands to unzip the binary and update file permission. Then move it to the system executable location (/usr/bin), as shown in Figures 8-7 and 8-8.

```
unzip nomad_${NOMAD_VERSION}_linux_amd64.zip
```

```
sudo chown root:root nomad
```

```
sudo mv nomad /usr/local/bin/
```

```
[root@ip-172-31-38-249 ~]# unzip nomad_${NOMAD_VERSION}_linux_amd64.zip
Archive:  nomad_1.0.1_linux_amd64.zip
  inflating: nomad
[root@ip-172-31-38-249 ~]# ls -lrt --color=never
total 143704
-rwxr-xr-x 1 root root 107707520 Dec 16 21:09 nomad
-rw-r--r-- 1 root root  39444296 Mar  8 00:58 nomad_1.0.1_linux_amd64.zip
[root@ip-172-31-38-249 ~]#
```

Figure 8-7. *Extracting Nomad binary from zip file*

```
[root@ip-172-31-38-249 ~]# sudo chown root:root nomad
[root@ip-172-31-38-249 ~]# ls -lrt --color=never
total 143704
-rwxr-xr-x 1 root root 107707520 Dec 16 21:09 nomad
-rw-r--r-- 1 root root  39444296 Mar  8 00:58 nomad_1.0.1_linux_amd64.zip
[root@ip-172-31-38-249 ~]# sudo mv nomad /usr/local/bin/
[root@ip-172-31-38-249 ~]#
```

Figure 8-8. *Moving Nomad binaries*

Execute the following command to verify the Nomad installation, as shown in Figure 8-9.

```
nomad version
```

```
[root@ip-172-31-38-249 ~]# nomad version
Nomad v1.0.1 (c9c68aa55a7275f22d2338f2df53e67ebfcb9238)
[root@ip-172-31-38-249 ~]#
```

Figure 8-9. *Verifying Nomad installation*

Execute the following commands to enable the autocompletion of Nomad commands, as shown in Figure 8-10.

```
nomad -autocomplete-install
```

```
complete -C /usr/local/bin/nomad nomad
```

```
[root@ip-172-31-38-249 ~]# nomad -autocomplete-install
[root@ip-172-31-38-249 ~]# complete -C /usr/local/bin/nomad nomad
[root@ip-172-31-38-249 ~]#
```

Figure 8-10. *Enabling autocompletion of Nomad commands*

Execute the following command to create an /opt/nomad data directory that stores Nomad service–related files. Check that the directory was created (see Figure 8-11).

```
mkdir -p /opt/nomad
```

```
file /opt/nomad
```

```
[root@ip-10-5-14-144 ~]# mkdir -p /opt/nomad
[root@ip-10-5-14-144 ~]# file /opt/nomad/
/opt/nomad/: directory
```

Figure 8-11. *Creating Nomad service file directory*

Create a Nomad service file called nomad.service in the /etc/systemd/ system directory, and add content using the files cloned in the first step (see Figure 8-12).

```
Sudo touch /etc/systemd/system/nomad.service
```

```
[root@ip-172-31-38-249 ~]# sudo touch /etc/systemd/system/nomad.service
[root@ip-172-31-38-249 ~]# █
```

Figure 8-12. *Creating Nomad service file*

Create a nomad.d directory in the /etc directory. Create nomad.hcl
and server.hcl server configuration files in the /etc/nomad.d directory
using the content of the cloned files (see Figure 8-13). The nomad.hcl file
provides information on the datacenter name (i.e., DC1) and the location
of the Nomad service directory (/opt/Nomad). The server.hcl file provides
the number of master nodes (i.e., 3).

```
sudo mkdir -parents /etc/nomad.d
```

```
sudo chmod 700 /etc/nomad.d
```

```
sudo touch /etc/nomad.d/server.hcl
```

```
[root@ip-172-31-38-249 ~]# sudo mkdir --parents /etc/nomad.d
[root@ip-172-31-38-249 ~]# sudo chmod 700 /etc/nomad.d
[root@ip-172-31-38-249 ~]# sudo touch /etc/nomad.d/nomad.hcl
[root@ip-172-31-38-249 ~]# █
```

```
[root@ip-172-31-38-249 ~]# sudo touch /etc/nomad.d/server.hcl
[root@ip-172-31-38-249 ~]# █
```

Figure 8-13. *Creating Nomad server configuration file*

Execute the following commands to enable and start the Nomad server
service, as shown in Figure 8-14.

```
sudo systemctl enable nomad
```

```
sudo systemctl start nomad
```

```
sudo systemctl status nomad
```

```
[root@ip-172-31-38-249 nomad.d]# sudo systemctl enable nomad
[root@ip-172-31-38-249 nomad.d]# sudo systemctl start nomad
[root@ip-172-31-38-249 nomad.d]# sudo systemctl status nomad
● nomad.service - Nomad
   Loaded: loaded (/etc/systemd/system/nomad.service; enabled; vendor preset: disabled)
   Active: active (running) since Mon 2021-03-08 01:18:25 UTC; 4s ago
     Docs: https://www.nomadproject.io/docs
 Main PID: 762 (nomad)
   CGroup: /system.slice/nomad.service
           └─762 /usr/local/bin/nomad agent -config /etc/nomad.d

Mar 08 01:18:25 ip-172-31-38-249.ec2.internal nomad[762]: 2021-03-08T01:18:25.726Z [INFO]  age....0
Mar 08 01:18:25 ip-172-31-38-249.ec2.internal nomad[762]: 2021-03-08T01:18:25.726Z [INFO]  age....0
Mar 08 01:18:25 ip-172-31-38-249.ec2.internal nomad[762]: 2021-03-08T01:18:25.736Z [INFO]  nom...[]
Mar 08 01:18:25 ip-172-31-38-249.ec2.internal nomad[762]: 2021-03-08T01:18:25.736Z [INFO]  nom...r=
Mar 08 01:18:25 ip-172-31-38-249.ec2.internal nomad[762]: 2021-03-08T01:18:25.737Z [INFO]  nom...49
Mar 08 01:18:25 ip-172-31-38-249.ec2.internal nomad[762]: 2021-03-08T01:18:25.737Z [INFO]  nom...e]
Mar 08 01:18:25 ip-172-31-38-249.ec2.internal nomad[762]: 2021-03-08T01:18:25.737Z [INFO]  nom...)"
Mar 08 01:18:25 ip-172-31-38-249.ec2.internal nomad[762]: 2021-03-08T01:18:25.738Z [ERROR] nom...d"
Mar 08 01:18:26 ip-172-31-38-249.ec2.internal nomad[762]: ==> Newer Nomad version available: 1...1)
Mar 08 01:18:27 ip-172-31-38-249.ec2.internal nomad[762]: 2021-03-08T01:18:27.585Z [WARN]  nom...on
Hint: Some lines were ellipsized, use -l to show in full.
[root@ip-172-31-38-249 nomad.d]# █
```

Figure 8-14. *Enabling Nomad server service*

Execute all the prior steps in this exercise on the other two Amazon Linux servers to set up a Nomad server component.

On the remaining two servers, join the two nodes with the leader. Execute the following command to register two Amazon Linux servers with the leader server (the first server set up), as shown in Figure 8-15.

```
nomad server join <IP Address of Nomad Leader Server(First
server we used in exercise)>:4648
```

```
[root@ip-172-31-38-249 nomad.d]# nomad server join 172.31.38.249:4648
Joined 1 servers successfully
[root@ip-172-31-38-249 nomad.d]# █
```

Figure 8-15. *Registering Nomad server with leader*

Execute the following command to verify the total members in the Nomad server, as shown in Figure 8-16.

```
nomad server members
```

```
[root@ip-172-31-33-110 ~]# nomad server join 172.31.38.249:4648
Joined 1 servers successfully
[root@ip-172-31-33-110 ~]# nomad server members
Name                                  Address         Port  Status  Leader  Protocol  Build  Datacenter  Region
ip-172-31-33-110.ec2.internal.global  172.31.33.110   4648  alive   true    2         1.0.1  dc1         global
ip-172-31-38-249.ec2.internal.global  172.31.38.249   4648  alive   false   2         1.0.1  dc1         global
ip-172-31-41-94.ec2.internal.global   172.31.41.94    4648  alive   false   2         1.0.1  dc1         global
[root@ip-172-31-33-110 ~]# ▮
```

Figure 8-16. *Listing Nomad server members*

You can review the Nomad server configuration in the UI. Navigate to http://<IP Address of Leader Nomad (the first server used in exercise)>:4646 to see your Nomad server configuration, as shown in Figure 8-17. Click Servers to review the three Nomad servers configured in the previous step.

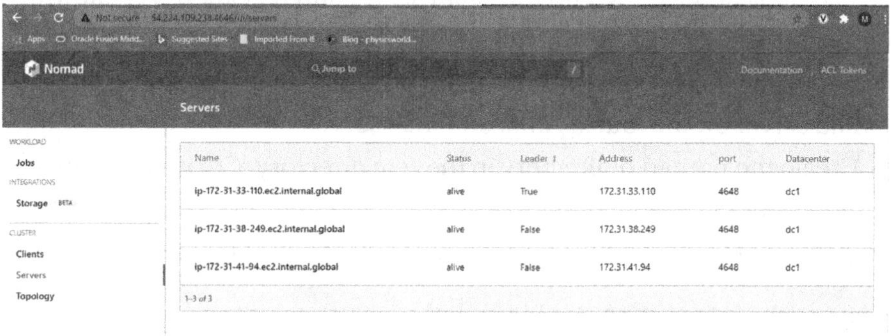

Figure 8-17. *Nomad UI server configuration*

Click Clients. You see that no clients are currently registered, as shown in Figure 8-18.

217

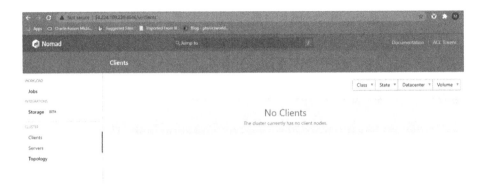

Figure 8-18. *Nomad UI client configuration*

Let's look at how to set up the client server and register the client with Nomad servers.

Repeat the first seven steps from the previous section to set up the Nomad server on the fourth Amazon Linux server.

Create the nomad.d directory in the /etc directory. Create the nomad. hcl and client.hcl client configuration files in the /etc/nomad.d directory using the content of the files cloned from GitHub (see Figure 8-19).

```
Sudo touch /etc/nomad.d/client.hcl
```

```
[root@ip-172-31-38-249 ~]# sudo touch /etc/nomad.d/client.hcl
[root@ip-172-31-38-249 ~]#
```

Figure 8-19. *Nomad client configuration*

Execute the following commands to enable and start the Nomad client service, as shown in Figure 8-20.

```
sudo systemctl enable nomad
```

```
sudo systemctl start nomad
```

```
sudo systemctl status nomad
```

```
[root@ip-172-31-38-249 nomad.d]# sudo systemctl enable nomad
[root@ip-172-31-38-249 nomad.d]# sudo systemctl start nomad
[root@ip-172-31-38-249 nomad.d]# sudo systemctl status nomad
● nomad.service - Nomad
   Loaded: loaded (/etc/systemd/system/nomad.service; enabled; vendor preset: disabled)
   Active: active (running) since Mon 2021-03-08 01:18:25 UTC; 4s ago
     Docs: https://www.nomadproject.io/docs
 Main PID: 762 (nomad)
   CGroup: /system.slice/nomad.service
           └─762 /usr/local/bin/nomad agent -config /etc/nomad.d

Mar 08 01:18:25 ip-172-31-38-249.ec2.internal nomad[762]: 2021-03-08T01:18:25.726Z [INFO]  age....0
Mar 08 01:18:25 ip-172-31-38-249.ec2.internal nomad[762]: 2021-03-08T01:18:25.726Z [INFO]  age....0
Mar 08 01:18:25 ip-172-31-38-249.ec2.internal nomad[762]: 2021-03-08T01:18:25.736Z [INFO]  nom...[]
Mar 08 01:18:25 ip-172-31-38-249.ec2.internal nomad[762]: 2021-03-08T01:18:25.736Z [INFO]  nom...r=
Mar 08 01:18:25 ip-172-31-38-249.ec2.internal nomad[762]: 2021-03-08T01:18:25.737Z [INFO]  nom...49
Mar 08 01:18:25 ip-172-31-38-249.ec2.internal nomad[762]: 2021-03-08T01:18:25.737Z [INFO]  nom...e]
Mar 08 01:18:25 ip-172-31-38-249.ec2.internal nomad[762]: 2021-03-08T01:18:25.737Z [INFO]  nom...)"
Mar 08 01:18:25 ip-172-31-38-249.ec2.internal nomad[762]: 2021-03-08T01:18:25.738Z [ERROR] nom...d"
Mar 08 01:18:26 ip-172-31-38-249.ec2.internal nomad[762]: ==> Newer Nomad version available: 1...1)
Mar 08 01:18:27 ip-172-31-38-249.ec2.internal nomad[762]: 2021-03-08T01:18:27.585Z [WARN]  nom...on
Hint: Some lines were ellipsized, use -l to show in full.
[root@ip-172-31-38-249 nomad.d]# █
```

Figure 8-20. *Enabling Nomad client service*

Now let's register the Nomad client with the Nomad server. Edit the client.hcl file in the /etc/nomad.d directory and add the information shown in Figure 8-21. The IP address field in the Servers section refers to the Nomad server IP address. TCP port 4647 is used for registration.

```
[root@ip-10-5-14-14 ~]# cat /etc/nomad.d/client.hcl
client {
  enabled = true
  servers = ["10.5.12.43:4647"]
}

acl {
  enabled = true
}

[root@ip-10-5-14-14 ~]# █
```

Figure 8-21. *Registering client with Nomad server*

Execute the following commands to restart and check the status of the Nomad client service, as shown in Figure 8-22.

```
sudo systemctl restart nomad
```

```
sudo systemctl status nomad
```

```
[root@ip-10-5-14-144 ~]# sudo systemctl restart nomad
[root@ip-10-5-14-144 ~]# sudo systemctl status nomad
● nomad.service - Nomad
   Loaded: loaded (/etc/systemd/system/nomad.service; enabled; vendor preset: disabled)
   Active: active (running) since Fri 2021-04-02 05:27:13 UTC; 56s ago
     Docs: https://www.nomadproject.io/docs
 Main PID: 5879 (nomad)
    Tasks: 8
   Memory: 16.2M
   CGroup: /system.slice/nomad.service
           └─5879 /usr/local/bin/nomad agent -config /etc/nomad.d

Apr 02 05:27:13 ip-10-5-14-144.ec2.internal nomad[5879]: 2021-04-02T05:27:13.671Z [INFO]  client.plugin: starting p...vice
Apr 02 05:27:13 ip-10-5-14-144.ec2.internal nomad[5879]: 2021-04-02T05:27:13.692Z [INFO]  client: started client: n...b593
Apr 02 05:27:15 ip-10-5-14-144.ec2.internal nomad[5879]: 2021-04-02T05:27:15.395Z [WARN]  nomad.raft: heartbeat tim...der=
Apr 02 05:27:15 ip-10-5-14-144.ec2.internal nomad[5879]: 2021-04-02T05:27:15.396Z [INFO]  nomad.raft: entering cand...rm=3
Apr 02 05:27:15 ip-10-5-14-144.ec2.internal nomad[5879]: 2021-04-02T05:27:15.401Z [INFO]  nomad.raft: election won:...ly=1
Apr 02 05:27:15 ip-10-5-14-144.ec2.internal nomad[5879]: 2021-04-02T05:27:15.401Z [INFO]  nomad.raft: entering lead...er)"
Apr 02 05:27:15 ip-10-5-14-144.ec2.internal nomad[5879]: 2021-04-02T05:27:15.402Z [INFO]  nomad: cluster leadership...ired
Apr 02 05:27:15 ip-10-5-14-144.ec2.internal nomad[5879]: 2021-04-02T05:27:15.452Z [INFO]  client: node registration...lete
Apr 02 05:27:18 ip-10-5-14-144.ec2.internal nomad[5879]: ==> Newer Nomad version available: 1.0.4 (currently runnin...0.1)
Apr 02 05:27:24 ip-10-5-14-144.ec2.internal nomad[5879]: 2021-04-02T05:27:24.111Z [INFO]  client: node registration...lete
Hint: Some lines were ellipsized, use -l to show in full.
[root@ip-10-5-14-144 ~]#
```

Figure 8-22. *Restart and check the status of Nomad client service*

Execute the following command to verify the Nomad client node status, as shown in Figure 8-23. A status-ready message indicates active clients. A status-down message indicates that the client is no longer available or is not reachable by the Nomad server.

```
nomad node status
```

```
[root@ip-10-5-14-14 ~]# nomad node status
ID        DC   Name                         Class    Drain  Eligibility  Status
d27a6cfa  dc1  ip-10-5-14-14.ec2.internal   <none>   false  eligible     ready
06453e06  dc1  ip-10-5-15-159.ec2.internal  <none>   false  eligible     down
```

Figure 8-23. *Verifying Nomad client*

You can review client details by navigating to the Nomad UI, as shown in Figure 8-24.

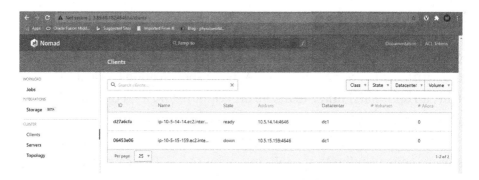

Figure 8-24. *Verifying Nomad client using UI*

Policy-Driven Governance in Nomad

Nomad's governance and policies capabilities let users address the complexity of a multi-team managed multi-cluster environment. Features like namespaces, resource quotas, Sentinel, and ACL help manage an environment in adherence to organizational standards. The governance and policy module is provided in the Enterprise version of Nomad. Let's look at how each of these capabilities help with application governance.

Namespaces

The Nomad namespaces feature allows a single cluster to be shared by many teams and projects without conflict. Nomad requires unique job IDs within namespaces, which allows each team to operate independently. When combined with ACLs, the isolation of namespaces can be enforced, allowing only designated users access to read or modify the jobs and associated objects in a namespace.

221

Resource Quotas

Within a namespace, resource quotas provide a mechanism for cluster administrators to restrict resources. A quota specification has a unique name, an optional human-readable description, and a set of limits. The quota limits define the allowed resource usage within a region.

When resource quotas are applied to a namespace, they limit resource consumption by the jobs in a namespace. This can prevent the consumption of excessive cluster resources and negatively impacting other teams or applications sharing the cluster.

Sentinel Policies

Sentinel policies use logic to enforce a certain resource requirement. Policies ensure that the resource request complies with user- or organization-defined policies. Sentinel policies declare a scope that determines when the policies apply. The only supported scope is "submit-job". This applies to any new jobs being submitted or existing jobs being updated (see Figure 8-25).

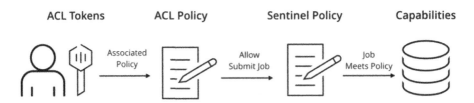

Figure 8-25. *Sentinel policies*

Sentinel policies support multiple enforcement levels, such as advisory, soft-mandatory, and hard mandatory. The advisory level emits a warning when the policy fails. Soft-mandatory and hard-mandatory prevent the operation. A soft-mandatory policy can be overridden if the user has the necessary permissions.

Nomad ACLs

Nomad provides an ACL feature that controls access to data or APIs. ACL policies are written using HashiCorp Configuration Language (HCL). ACL comprises four key objects to govern resource access policies.

Tokens

Requests to Nomad are authenticated using a bearer token. Each ACL token has a public accessor ID that names a token and a secret ID to make requests to Nomad. The secret ID is provided using a request header (X-Nomad-Token) and authenticates the caller. Tokens are management or client types. The management tokens effectively "root" in the system and can perform any operation. The client tokens are associated with one or more ACL policies that grant specific capabilities.

Policies

Policies consist of a set of rules defining the capabilities or actions to be granted. For example, a read-only policy might only grant the ability to list and inspect running jobs but not submit new ones. No permissions are granted by default, making Nomad a default-deny system.

Rules

Policies are comprised of one or more rules. The rules define the capabilities of a Nomad ACL token for accessing objects in a cluster—like namespaces, node, agent, operator, quota. The full set of rules are discussed later.

Capabilities

Capabilities are a set of actions that can be performed. This includes listing jobs, submitting jobs, and querying nodes. A management token is granted all capabilities. Client tokens are granted specific capabilities via ACL policies. The full set of capabilities is discussed in the rule specifications.

Container Application Deployment Using Nomad

Now let's perform a hands-on exercise to deploy a containerized application using Nomad. We begin by setting up Docker on the Nomad client server.

Execute the following commands to install and start Docker on the Nomad client server, as shown in Figures 8-26, 8-27, 8-28, and 8-29. Nomad automatically detects the installed Docker components using its drivers.

```
sudo yum update -y
sudo amazon-linux-extras install docker
systemctl start docker
systemctl status docker
```

```
[root@ip-10-5-14-144 ~]# sudo yum update -y
Loaded plugins: extras_suggestions, langpacks, priorities, update-motd
No packages marked for update
[root@ip-10-5-14-144 ~]#
```

Figure 8-26. *Update all the installed packages.*

```
[root@ip-10-5-14-144 ~]# sudo amazon-linux-extras install docker
Installing docker
Loaded plugins: extras_suggestions, langpacks, priorities, update-motd
Cleaning repos: amzn2-core amzn2extra-docker
12 metadata files removed
4 sqlite files removed
0 metadata files removed
Loaded plugins: extras_suggestions, langpacks, priorities, update-motd
amzn2-core                                                                    | 3.7 kB  00:00:00
amzn2extra-docker                                                             | 3.0 kB  00:00:00
(1/5): amzn2-core/2/x86_64/updateinfo                                         | 362 kB  00:00:00
(2/5): amzn2-core/2/x86_64/group_gz                                           | 2.5 kB  00:00:00
(3/5): amzn2extra-docker/2/x86_64/updateinfo                                  |  76 B   00:00:00
(4/5): amzn2extra-docker/2/x86_64/primary_db                                  |  76 kB  00:00:00
(5/5): amzn2-core/2/x86_64/primary_db                                         |  51 MB  00:00:01
Resolving Dependencies
--> Running transaction check
---> Package docker.x86_64 0:19.03.13ce-1.amzn2 will be installed
--> Processing Dependency: runc >= 1.0.0 for package: docker-19.03.13ce-1.amzn2.x86_64
--> Processing Dependency: containerd >= 1.3.2 for package: docker-19.03.13ce-1.amzn2.x86_64
--> Processing Dependency: pigz for package: docker-19.03.13ce-1.amzn2.x86_64
--> Processing Dependency: libcgroup for package: docker-19.03.13ce-1.amzn2.x86_64
--> Running transaction check
---> Package containerd.x86_64 0:1.4.4-1.amzn2 will be installed
---> Package libcgroup.x86_64 0:0.41-21.amzn2 will be installed
Running transaction
  Installing : runc-1.0.0-0.1.20210225.git12644e6.amzn2.x86_64                                 1/5
  Installing : containerd-1.4.4-1.amzn2.x86_64                                                 2/5
  Installing : libcgroup-0.41-21.amzn2.x86_64                                                  3/5
  Installing : pigz-2.3.4-1.amzn2.0.1.x86_64                                                   4/5
  Installing : docker-19.03.13ce-1.amzn2.x86_64                                                5/5
  Verifying  : containerd-1.4.4-1.amzn2.x86_64                                                 1/5
  Verifying  : docker-19.03.13ce-1.amzn2.x86_64                                                2/5
  Verifying  : runc-1.0.0-0.1.20210225.git12644e6.amzn2.x86_64                                 3/5
  Verifying  : pigz-2.3.4-1.amzn2.0.1.x86_64                                                   4/5
  Verifying  : libcgroup-0.41-21.amzn2.x86_64                                                  5/5

Installed:
  docker.x86_64 0:19.03.13ce-1.amzn2
```

Figure 8-27. *Installing Docker on Nomad client server*

```
[root@ip-10-5-14-144 ~]# systemctl start docker
```

Figure 8-28. *Start Docker service on Nomad client server*

```
[root@ip-172-31-47-200 ~]# systemctl status docker
● docker.service - Docker Application Container Engine
   Loaded: loaded (/usr/lib/systemd/system/docker.service; disabled; vendor preset: disabled)
   Active: active (running) since Mon 2021-03-08 02:24:38 UTC; 4min 11s ago
     Docs: https://docs.docker.com
  Process: 5818 ExecStartPre=/usr/libexec/docker/docker-setup-runtimes.sh (code=exited, status=0/SUCC
  Process: 5807 ExecStartPre=/bin/mkdir -p /run/docker (code=exited, status=0/SUCCESS)
 Main PID: 5825 (dockerd)
    Tasks: 10
   Memory: 38.3M
   CGroup: /system.slice/docker.service
           └─5825 /usr/bin/dockerd -H fd:// --containerd=/run/containerd/containerd.sock --default-ul

Mar 08 02:24:34 ip-172-31-47-200.ec2.internal dockerd[5825]: time="2021-03-08T02:24:34.766990442Z" le
Mar 08 02:24:34 ip-172-31-47-200.ec2.internal dockerd[5825]: time="2021-03-08T02:24:34.767262226Z" le
Mar 08 02:24:34 ip-172-31-47-200.ec2.internal dockerd[5825]: time="2021-03-08T02:24:34.767560423Z" le
Mar 08 02:24:38 ip-172-31-47-200.ec2.internal dockerd[5825]: time="2021-03-08T02:24:38.387135900Z" le
Mar 08 02:24:38 ip-172-31-47-200.ec2.internal dockerd[5825]: time="2021-03-08T02:24:38.664944090Z" le
Mar 08 02:24:38 ip-172-31-47-200.ec2.internal dockerd[5825]: time="2021-03-08T02:24:38.850045050Z" le
Mar 08 02:24:38 ip-172-31-47-200.ec2.internal dockerd[5825]: time="2021-03-08T02:24:38.880421734Z" le
Mar 08 02:24:38 ip-172-31-47-200.ec2.internal dockerd[5825]: time="2021-03-08T02:24:38.880524590Z" le
Mar 08 02:24:38 ip-172-31-47-200.ec2.internal systemd[1]: Started Docker Application Container Engine
```

Figure 8-29. *Check the status of Docker service on Nomad client server*

You can verify the installation from the Nomad UI, as shown in Figure 8-30. Navigate to the Client section and click the client name to view the details of the Docker installation.

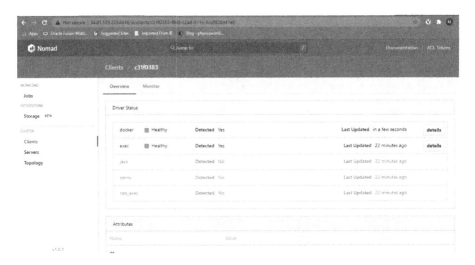

Figure 8-30. *Verifying Docker installation using Nomad UI*

The Easy Travel application is used for this hands-on exercise. It is a multi-tier application built using microservices principles. The application simulates issues such as high CPU load, database slowdowns, or slow authentication problems. Figure 8-31 is an architectural diagram of the application. We installed only the customer frontend portion, including Nginx, a frontend and backend database, and a load generator.

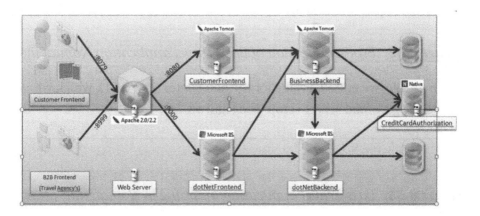

Figure 8-31. *Easy Travel application architecture*

Table 8-2 describes the components in the Easy Travel application.

Table 8-2. *Application Components*

Component	Description
Mongodb	A pre-populated travel database (MongoDB)
Backend	The Easy Travel business backend (Java)
Frontend	The Easy Travel customer frontend (Java)
Nginx	A reverse-proxy for the Easy Travel customer frontend
Loadgen	A synthetic UEM load generator (Java)

Earlier in this chapter, we cloned a few files from GitHub. We used a file named easytravel.nomad, which contains the configuration for the Easy Travel application. Let's look at the various sections in the file.

The Easy Travel application consists of five microservices that are defined as different groups in easytravel.nomad. Each group contains a configuration related to its microservice. Figure 8-32 shows the block used for the frontend.

```
# - frontend #
group "frontend" {
```

Figure 8-32. *Frontend section of Easy Travel application Nomad file*

In the file, we added a value for the datacenter (i.e., DC1), which we used during Nomad server setup (see Figure 8-33).

```
[root@ip-10-5-12-43 ~]# cat easytravel.nomad █
job "easytraveltest1" {
  datacenters = ["dc1"]
```

Figure 8-33. *Easy Travel application mapping to Nomad datacenter*

The file also contains a constraint section. Defining constraints is optional because it restricts the deployment to specific clients based on OS type, kernel version, IP address, and so forth. Our example uses Linux as the kernel value since we use an Amazon Linux EC2 instance to run the Easy Travel application (see Figure 8-34).

```
constraint {
  attribute = "${attr.kernel.name}"
  value = "linux"
}
```

Figure 8-34. *Constraint section in Nomad deployment file*

The Group section within the easytravel.nomad file has the following subsections, as shown in Figure 8-35.

- **count**: The number of containers to be deployed.

- **network**: Defines the ports for microservices communication.

- **restart**: Nomad periodically checks the health status of deployed containers and reinitiates the task in the event of a failure.

- **task**: Defines the resources to be consumed like CPU, RAM, and the image to build a container.

```
count = 1
network {
port "http" {
  to = 8080
}
}
restart {
  attempts = 10
  interval = "5m"
  delay = "25s"
  mode = "delay"
}
```

Figure 8-35. *Group section in Nomad deployment file*

Execute the following command to validate the easytravel.nomad
file for any syntax errors and a dry-run of the Easy Travel application
deployment, as shown in Figure 8-36.

```
nomad job plan easytravel.nomad
```

```
[root@ip-10-5-12-43 ~]# nomad job plan easytravel.nomad
 Job: "easytraveltest1"
+ Task Group: "backend" (1 create)
  + Task: "easytravel-backend" (forces create)

+ Task Group: "frontend" (1 create)
  + Task: "easytravel-frontend" (forces create)

+ Task Group: "loadgen" (1 create)
  + Task: "easytravel-loadgen" (forces create)

+ Task Group: "mongodb" (1 create)
  + Task: "easytravel-mongodb" (forces create)

+ Task Group: "nginx" (1 create)
  + Task: "easytravel-nginx" (forces create)

Scheduler dry-run:
- All tasks successfully allocated.

Job Modify Index: 0
To submit the job with version verification run:

nomad job run -check-index 0 easytravel.nomad
```

Figure 8-36. *Easy Travel deployment dry run*

Execute the following command to deploy the Easy Travel application,
as shown in Figure 8-37.

```
nomad job run easytravel.nomad
```

```
  [new] 226c, 3717c written
[root@ip-10-5-12-43 ~]# nomad job run easytravel.nomad
==> Monitoring evaluation "ebef11d2"
    Evaluation triggered by job "easytraveltest1"
==> Monitoring evaluation "ebef11d2"
    Evaluation within deployment: "cbd40c8e"
    Allocation "2296fdb4" created: node "d27a6cfa", group "backend"
    Allocation "2707d210" created: node "d27a6cfa", group "frontend"
    Allocation "2f2d4d6f" created: node "d27a6cfa", group "mongodb"
    Allocation "7772bfe8" created: node "d27a6cfa", group "loadgen"
    Allocation "e1d0feae" created: node "d27a6cfa", group "nginx"
    Evaluation status changed: "pending" -> "complete"
==> Evaluation "ebef11d2" finished with status "complete"
[root@ip-10-5-12-43 ~]# 
```

Figure 8-37. *Easy Travel deployment dry run*

Once the deployment job is completed, you can review the application configuration in the Nomad UI. Navigate to the Jobs section and click the Easy Travel job to view details, as shown in Figure 8-38.

Figure 8-38. *Easy Travel configuration review from Nomad UI*

In the Nomad UI, you can see the number of containers deployed in each group and their health status, as shown in Figure 8-39.

Figure 8-39. *Easy Travel container health status*

You can drill down the Nomad UI to see the details of all the
containers, as shown in Figure 8-40.

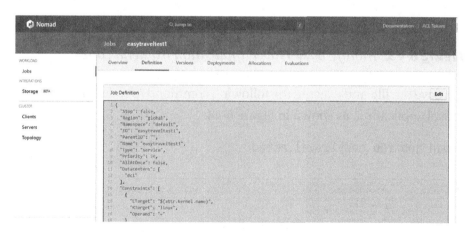

Figure 8-40. *Easy Travel container health status*

The Definition tab provides information on the application deployed
using the easytravel.nomad file (see Figure 8-41).

Figure 8-41. *Easy Travel application definition*

Nomad captures the job versions if you update code multiple times
for the same job, as shown in Figure 8-42. It also allows you to revert to a
specific version.

Figure 8-42. *Easy Travel application versioning*

Let's try to modify the Easy Travel application and see how Nomad reports the changes. Edit the easytravel.nomad file by changing the frontend count to 2, as shown in Figure 8-43.

```
###################################################################################
# - frontend #
group "frontend" {
  count = 2
  network {
  port "http" {
    to = 8080
  }
```

Figure 8-43. *Modify Easy Travel application frontend count*

Save the file and execute the following command to redeploy the Easy Travel application, as shown in Figure 8-44.

```
nomad job run easytravel.nomad
```

```
[root@ip-10-5-12-43 ~]# nomad job run easytravel.nomad
==> Monitoring evaluation "13627b78"
    Evaluation triggered by job "easytraveltest1"
==> Monitoring evaluation "13627b78"
    Evaluation within deployment: "2377e980"
    Allocation "1c2b0c97" created: node "d27a6cfa", group "frontend"
    Allocation "2296fdb4" modified: node "d27a6cfa", group "backend"
    Allocation "2707d210" modified: node "d27a6cfa", group "frontend"
    Allocation "2f2d4d6f" modified: node "d27a6cfa", group "mongodb"
    Allocation "7772bfe8" modified: node "d27a6cfa", group "loadgen"
    Allocation "e1d0feae" modified: node "d27a6cfa", group "nginx"
    Evaluation status changed: "pending" -> "complete"
==> Evaluation "13627b78" finished with status "complete"
```

Figure 8-44. *Redeploy Easy Travel application*

You can review the configuration in the Jobs section of the Nomad UI. Click the Versions tab, as shown in Figure 8-45. You can see the changes made to the Easy Travel application.

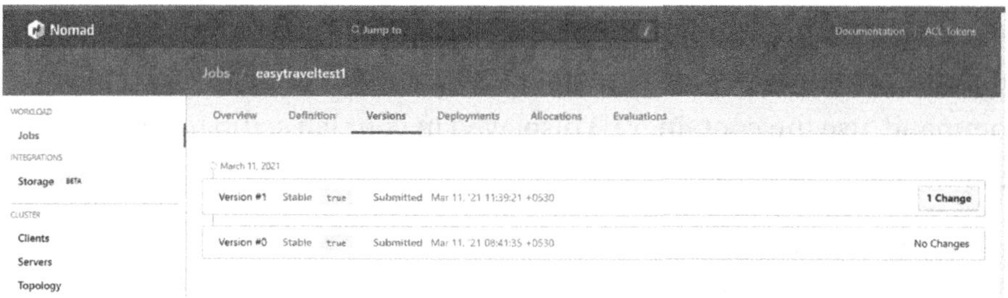

Figure 8-45. *Review Easy Travel application change history*

You can review the resources allocated to the deployed containers by navigating to the Allocations tab. It shows the allocated CPU and memory for each container (see Figure 8-46). The CPU and Memory bars in the far-right columns are continuously updated as they gather information from a Nomad client.

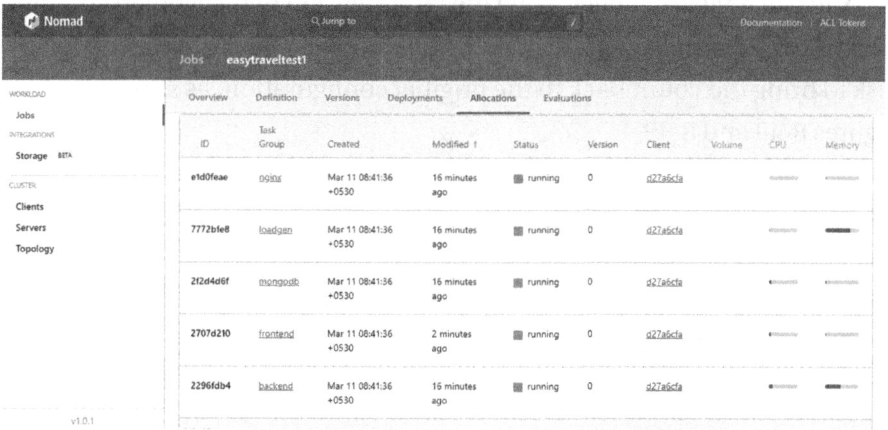

Figure 8-46. *Allocation detail for Easy Travel application*

233

Nomad initiates self-healing tasks in the event of a failure. To test this scenario, let's stop one of the containers by using the docker command, as shown in Figure 8-47. Once the container is stopped, Nomad automatically brings it back to the desired running state. The first command lists the container ID running on the Nomad client server. The second command stops the container per the container ID. While executing the second command, use the container ID displayed in your lab setup to view the results.

```
docker container ls -aq
```

```
docker container stop <Container ID>
```

```
[root@ip-10-5-14-14 ~]# docker container ls -aq
6296d04e7711
b9dead21a304
9647757e3f13
f4938ecc322b
8d1457635510
[root@ip-10-5-14-14 ~]# docker container stop 8d1457635510
8d1457635510
[root@ip-10-5-14-14 ~]#
```

Figure 8-47. *Stopping Easy Travel application container*

You can review changes using the Overview tab in the Nomad UI. After stopping the running container, the count reduces. Nomad triggers the task to bring the count back to the original configuration, as shown in Figures 8-48 and 8-49.

Figure 8-48. *Easy Travel application container count after stopping container*

Figure 8-49. *Easy Travel application container count after self-healing*

You can review the changes to the stopped container by clicking the container ID, as shown in Figure 8-50.

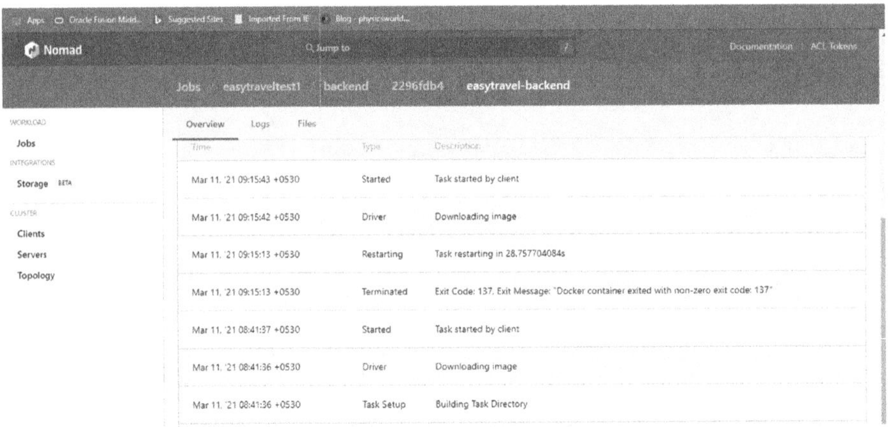

Figure 8-50. Easy Travel application container change history

Summary

This chapter covered the main concepts of HashiCorp Nomad. We learned how to install open source Nomad. We also performed a hands-on exercise in application deployment using Nomad.

With this we have reached the end of our journey on Infrastructure as code using various tools from Hashicorp. We hope that you have enjoyed the journey and learnt the basics of these tools and will progress to deploy and use them in your environments.

Index

V, W, X, Y, Z